Reading Disability
Experiment, Innovation
and Individual Therapy

M. S. JACKSON

ANGUS AND ROBERTSON

First published in 1972 by

ANGUS AND ROBERTSON (PUBLISHERS) PTY LTD

102 Glover Street, Cremorne, Sydney
2 Fisher Street, London
107 Elizabeth Street, Melbourne
167 Queen Street, Brisbane
89 Anson Road, Singapore

© M. S. Jackson

National Library of Australia
card number and ISBN 0 207 12366 7

Registered in Australia for transmission by post as a book
PRINTED IN AUSTRALIA BY WATSON FERGUSON AND CO, BRISBANE

Reading Disability
Experiment, Innovation
and Individual Therapy

This book is dedicated to the many
unfortunate and disabled readers
I have encountered and to their
aid and assistance.

Preface

This book comprises five reports of educational therapeutic work done with reading disabled children.

Reports 1, 2 and 3 describe innovatory procedures practised with individual children. Report No. 2 describes an experiment with a group of young children who in their second year at school had made scarcely any progress in reading.

These current studies in educational and therapeutic practice were commenced in 1967 at Monash University. They are an extension of work commenced by the author in 1947.

The procedures described, while specifically designed to aid severely disabled readers (dyslexics), have also been found to be most beneficial to ordinary children, and it is recommended that these innovatory procedures be incorporated into the practice of the everyday classroom.

The approach described in Report No. 1 is particularly suited to the secondary school pupil who is failing. The apparatus described in Report No. 2 has been used with success not only to assist in reading but also to teach spelling at all levels including adult disabled readers.

Contents

DON, A CASE OF CHRONIC DYSLEXIA: THERAPY AND TREATMENT

Don, a case of chronic dyslexia: therapy and treatment

At almost thirteen years of age Don was a tall, good-looking boy with a clear, slightly swarthy complexion. He had natural wavy hair and brown eyes, but a rather sad and melancholy look of depression. At least part of the explanation for this expression lay in the fact that for all his school life he had made virtually no progress in one of the most socially valued communication skills which everybody seemed to possess: the skill of reading. Although tall and good-looking, seemingly intelligent and with good ability in most other areas, and although now in the final year of the primary school, Don was reading like a child of five and a half or six years of age at most.

PRENATAL AND EARLY HISTORY

There was a prenatal history of chronic toxicity. The delivery was brought on at eight months after the mother had been ill for most of the gestation period. In addition she was in labour for about twelve hours.

There was no history of poor reading in the family. The neurologist who examined the boy felt quite certain that his condition was due to minimal brain damage sustained during the prenatal and perhaps paranatal period.

Don walked at an average age and the mother could not think of any early difficulties such as bed-wetting, thumb-sucking or feeding problems, or signs of emotional disturbance. In fact, he was described by his mother as a good boy.

The father, a member of the permanent army, was sent to the Middle East when Don was three and a half. The wife accompanied her husband and an attempt was made to send the boy to the school near where the family was located. The mother reported the child was terrified and would "go down on his knees and plead with her not to take him to school". She persisted for several months, then relented. He was four years of age at that time.

The family returned to Australia and the boy was sent to the nearest state school at five years of age. He made no progress at school in reading ability, though he was average at mathematics and, as he got older, excelled as an athlete. He won the swimming events at the school sports annually. The teachers reported that he was no bother in school and was good at many things.

The mother felt the child was intelligent but was either lazy or stupid somehow. In describing her own attitude to her son's disability the mother said she was puzzled, and in attempting to get him to do well in his reading she became exasperated and often lost her temper, after which she would then try encouragement. This pattern of alternating reactions on the part of the mother played a major part in the boy's self-evaluation throughout his entire school history. As a reaction to this behaviour on the part of his parents, he became intensely frustrated. This frustration was obvious: he would sigh heavily, and hold his breath, and he would become bad-tempered and moody. His father, who was away from home a good deal, was highly disappointed in his son, and was described by the mother as having "broken his heart over the boy". There were two brothers, eight and ten years older than Don respectively, who were described as perfectly normal; however they lived away from home, near where they were working.

As a consequence of the frequent absence of the father and other sons, the mother leaned on Don for a good deal of assistance about the house with the chores. It was in this relationship that she found him to be "most helpful"; "a good kid" who would "do anything for you." Nevertheless, she expressed her mystification over her son by saying: "I don't know, he seems intelligent, but he just can't read".

Don came to the clinic at Monash after this long history of frustration and school failure, and numerous attempts by the parents to find a solution to his problem. When he learned that he was coming, and that there was some chance that someone might be able to help him, his mother reported that he was counting the days off on the calendar.

THE NATURE OF DON'S PROBLEM

Don was of average intelligence. On the Wechsler Intelligence Test his I.Q. was 101; and when looked at more closely, there was very little difference between his verbal I.Q. of 103 on that scale and his performance I.Q. of 99 on the same test.

The following information was obtained from two well-known standard reading tests.
1. Results on the Schonell (1960) Diagnostic Attainment Reading Tests:

	Reading Age
(a) the graded word reading test	5 years 7 months
(b) the comprehension reading test	6 years
(c) the oral reading test	6 years
(d) silent reading test	6 years

2. His reading age on the Daniels and Diack (1960) Standard Reading Test was 6 years. He had chronic letter and word reversals and confusions; the letters b and d were particularly troublesome to him.
Don's responses to the words in the left-hand column are listed on the right:

Word to be read	*Don's Reading Response*
barn	broom
yarn	yawn
seek	skin
tent	test
bird	bird
house	horse
rag	rig
glad	gold
we	me

An examination of his responses indicate that he had some knowledge of sounds but made wild stabs at most words. He managed the initial sound in all but one instance.

An examination of Don's responses on the Illinois Test of Psycholinguistic Abilities indicates that those areas of ability necessary for reading behaviour were poorly developed. In particular in the visual motor sequencing and visual motor association tests he appeared to be functioning like a child just about to commerce school.

Don's responses on the I.T.P.A. Test:

Test	*Language*
Auditory-Vocal Automatic Test	6.1
Visual Decoding Test	6.10
Motor Encoding Test	8.3
Auditory-Vocal Association Test	8.3
Visual Motor Sequencing Test	4.2
Vocal Encoding Test	5.8
Auditory-Vocal Sequencing Test	7.0
Visual Motor Association Test	4.7
Auditory Decoding Test	8.10
I.T.P.A. Total:	9.4

OTHER DISABILITIES

Impoverishment of concepts and ideas, with inability to sequence

This was well illustrated when Don was shown a picture and asked first to tell what was happening in the picture and then to give it a name. The test procedure was as follows: Don was shown a colour picture of some young Indonesian fishermen sitting and standing around on some rocks by the sea. The following dialogue ensued between the therapist and child:

T. "Tell me something about the picture".
D. "Some kids sitting around".
T. "What do you think they are talking about?"
D. "That they are being photographed".
T. "What nationality are the people?"
D. "The kids that they are".

T.   "What nationality or race do you think they are, and what are they doing?"
D.   "The Indian kids that they are sitting on the rocks".
T.   "Does that make sense?"
D.   "Yes".
T.   "Try again".
D.   "The Indian kids are sitting on the rocks".
T.   "Yes, what are they doing?"
D.   "Talking".
T.   "What about?"
D.   "Being photographed".
T.   "Say something about their dress".
D.   "Rags".
T.   "Put that into a sentence".
D.   No response.
T.   "Tell me about what they are wearing. Can you say something to get an idea started?"
D.   "Torn and ragged".
T.   "Now put that into a sentence".
D.   "Their clothes are torn and rags".
T.   "Good".

When asked to give a name to the picture he just shrugged.

A comparison of different modes of response to verbal stimuli

The Daniels and Diack Graded Spelling Test was administered and Don was asked to respond in three different ways, merely to observe consistency in response modes:
(a) by orally spelling the word,
(b) by composing the word and using plastic letters of the alphabet, and
(c) by writing the word on paper.

TABLE 1.1: Don's responses to the Daniels and Diack Graded Spelling Test

The word dictated by therapist	Orally spelt	Composing words with plastic letters of alphabet	Writing word
eye	in	in	in
fight	fiot	fit	firt
friend	fren	fand	frend
done	dan	dan	dane
any	one	any	ane
great	gat	gate	grat
sure	shor	sare	sare
women	wommen	wommen	women
answer	ans	ners	anare
beautiful	butfal	dutfull	dutfull

Don's ability to express himself in writing

This has already been demonstrated when Don was asked to spell certain words. In an effort to find one of his main interests, however, he was asked what he had done over the weekend. He explained that he had made a flying fox. He was then given a sheet of paper to
  (a) draw what this looked like (his responses are indicated in Figure 1.1:),

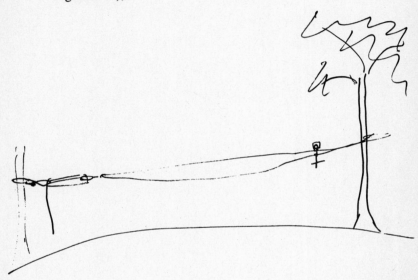

FIGURE 1.1

and (b) to write out how he had made it. His attempt to write it revealed four major problems which confronted him:
1. a thought sequencing problem;
2. an inability to encode the words which he wanted to use;
3. an inability to put a sufficient number of words down to make sense; that is, he omitted noun markers, joining words and indeed whole blocks of words, which made it completely incomprehensible;
4. an inability to read back what he had written.
His written attempt is reproduced in Figure 1.2.
  Don's oral account follows and reveals clearly quite a sophisticated level of intellectual and engineering functioning.

Don's oral account of how to make a flying fox

  "You get a piece of rope and you tie it on a tree, first you put a pulley or block in the middle of it, then you get another pulley and tie it onto

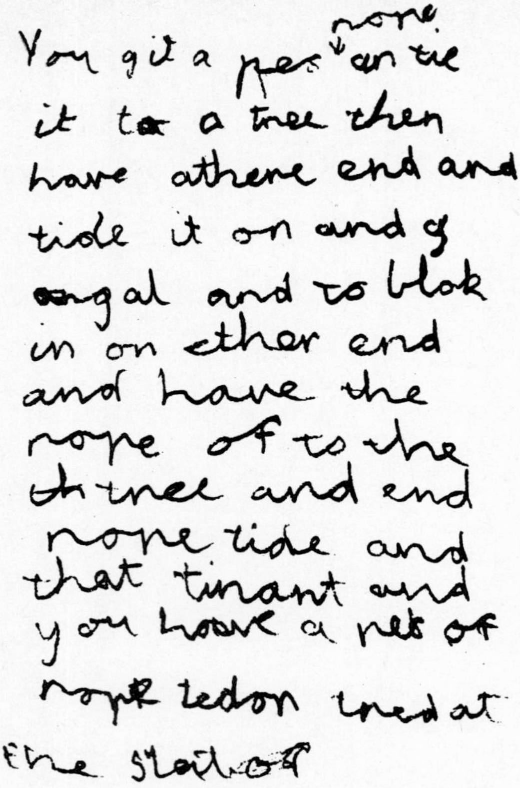

You git a pers'an tie
it ta a tree then
have athene end and
tide it on and g
ong al and to blok
in on ether end
and have the
rope of to the
th tree and end
none tide and
that tinant and
you have a net of
rope ledon tred at
the sterlot

FIGURE 1.2

the hook of the pulley, and you thread it up with the other pulley and the other tree, you put a sling around the branch and then you put it on the hook of the other pulley and the rope that hangs from the pulley; you pull down on it to make it tight and the pulley that's been in the middle you tie a piece of rope on the pulley and get up to the highest part of the flying fox and go down on it".

Don's own perception of his disability

Of his disability he commented: "Sometimes I can read, sometimes I can't". "My eyes drop down and I can't find the place for a couple of minutes". "My worst subject is reading and spelling". "In an English lesson two weeks ago I was looking at a word and the word just turned green. Sometimes it goes starry for 15 seconds".

He was righthanded and remarked, "I always write with my right hand", although he showed the usual confusion when asked "which is your right hand", "show your left hand", and the like.

On a self-rating scale about reading, Don selected the following responses from a multiple-choice questionnaire:
1.   I rate myself as a person who: "tries very hard to read".
2.   I would rate my ability to read as: "below average".
3.   I would rate my reading teacher as: "very good".
4.   When the work at school gets difficult I: "give up after a while".

THE RATIONALE AND THEORY OF THE EDUCATIONAL THERAPEUTIC PROGRAMME DESIGNED FOR DON

One of the central problems in teaching backward readers to read lies in the fact that such a person lacks ideas about which to think, talk and subsequently read. There appears to be a lack of focalization on any specific theme for a sufficiently long period to sustain a sequence of ideas.

Most writers would take the view that the job of translating ideas, which are already in the memory system, into visual symbols is not nearly so difficult as the task of firstly generating ideas, then getting them into the central nervous system and consequently translating them into visual symbols.

The method to be described here was designed by the author to cope with problems such as those expressed by Don. It has been called the visuo-thematic approach to the teaching of reading and language to reading disability cases. It is not a new method such as phonics or "look and say"; it is simply a proposal for integrating and organising the reading of the dyslexic child around a focal point.

Gibson (1966) makes the point that there are several ways of chacterizing the reading process, one of which is getting meaning from the printed page.

The core of the proposal put forward here is that children derive meaning from the printed page to the extent that *they* put meaning into it; and the proposal which follows is an attempt to explicate this point.

The procedure to be adopted in this presentation will be to describe the method and its rationale; to illustrate its operation with Don, who clearly is a case of chronic dyslexia; and then to explain the case results in terms of a conceptual model.

The term dyslexia as used here is not the sense in which Critchley (1964) has used it, though the actual case used to illustrate the procedure is one of the worst known to the author, and would be of the symptom variety referred to by Critchley. The dispute over definition is nicely considered by Reid (1968) and will not be considered here, except to say that the term as used here denotes that group of children who are generally considered to be of at least average intellect and who have extreme difficulty in learning to read for a variety of reasons.

The Method and its Rationale

The visuo-thematic approach consists of presenting the child (or adult) with a visual stimulus which has a sufficient number of ideas in it to generate discussion and to eventually "suggest" a story without too much imagination being required. The visual stimuli which have been chosen for this approach are the Salt Bush Bill pictures and Witchetty's Tribe pictures.[1] One of these, Figure 1.3, will provide the focus for this present discussion.

The rationale for choosing such pictures is as follows:

1. the pictures present, on a regular weekly basis, a set of stable characters which can be given names by the child and which can thereafter be consistently used;

2. the pictures present an endless variety of ideas around certain broad themes, namely, life in the country, or the life of Aboriginals. Thus variety and stability are present at the same time, as a constant frame of reference from which to draw concepts and subsequently the visual equivalents of the concepts used (i.e., to read);

3. it is assumed that personal involvement, participation, insight and overall planning fosters learning and is of much higher reward value than more passive forms of reading instruction. In this context the child has to participate by acquiring at least one picture per week and by building up a set of appropriate vocabulary, a subsequent story and his own set of questions about the story. In this way the child has his own permanent record for revision purposes. Critchley (1964) has observed that dyslexic children have a fondness for building up and taking apart mechanical models. Maybe the "mechanical" aspects of preparing the picture and assembling the words thereon is not too remotely removed from such a concept. Bruner (1966) has also observed that children learn better when they do participate;

4. it is assumed that one particular thematic environment will eventually be relatively saturated and provide a stepping stone to a different theme;

5. a further assumption of this method is that thinking, reading, writing, spelling and concept formation are all interdependent factors, each one aiding the development of the other. This assumption has received some support from Gattegno (1962), Bloomfield (1963) and others who have argued that reading, writing and spelling are reciprocally reinforcing and are all different expressions of the one basic function of reading or information extraction;

6. yet another assumption underlying this method is that the material lends itself to some forms of creativity. The first of these forms is deciding what words to use, the second is the making up of sentences and stories about the picture, the third is the giving of a title to the picture and finally writing and answering questions that can be asked about the picture.

---

[1] These pictures occur weekly in *Pix* magazine. Figure 1.3 is reproduced by kind permission of Eric Jolliffe.

The Procedure

The child obtains the picture which he pastes on a thin piece of cardboard together with a matchbox in the corner of the picture which is to be used for housing all the words the child can think of to describe various aspects of the picture. This is useful for instant revision of vocabulary from time to time.

The child is required to have three columns ruled on a page headed, respectively, *naming words, describing words* and *action words*. He is then asked to try to think of at least six words which can be placed in each of the above columns, thus giving a total of at least 18 words for the picture. He writes the words out at home (or in therapy) in their appropriate columns, and he is also asked to put each word on a small strip of cardboard and place it in the matchbox. Thus a library of pictures and their respective vocabularies is built up by the child. When the child comes to the lesson (if the above is done at home) the teacher therapist checks the words for accuracy and the child's ability to recognize them. He is then given some word building (or spelling) of the words, using the Merrill Jackson Structured Alphabet (Jackson, 1969).

The next step is for the child to construct his own series of questions about aspects of the picture and leave them open to be answered at the teaching session.

Then the child is asked to write a story about the picture and give it a title. The story is read over by the child together with the therapist and any corrections noted. After this the child is asked to re-write the story (or type it if he can) in its final form, and to paste it in a book beside the vocabulary which has also been handled in this fashion.

This procedure is repeated at least once a week, using on each occasion a different story but the same format and structure. Thus the child builds up a stable set of expectations and techniques for coping with the task of language development, of which reading is only a part.

An account of an actual session:

The session to be described was one which occurred after he had been in therapy for 26 hours. The sessions were conducted weekly and were of one hour's duration. Don was required, however, to do a considerable amount of personal preparation for each session.

For Session 26, Don came with the picture shown in Figure 1.3 and the words displayed in Table 1.2, together with the story (Figure 1.4) and questions which he composed.

TABLE 1.2: The words used by Don to describe the pictures

Doing words (verbs)	Naming words (nouns)	Describing words (adjectives)
shining	fire	brown
talking	spear	black
burning	log	
	snake	

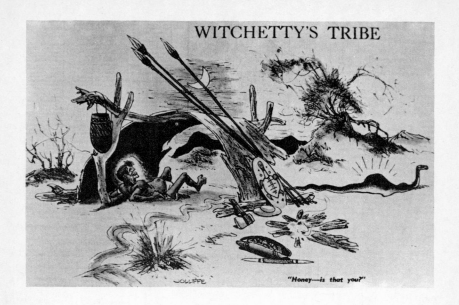

WITCHETTY'S TRIBE

"Honey—is that you?"

FIGURE 1.3

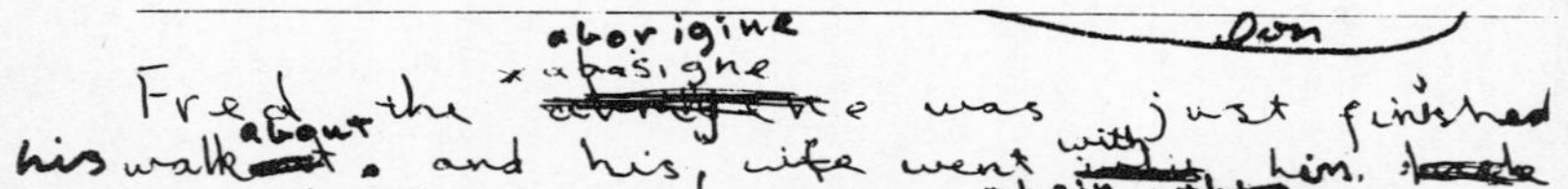

aborigine
×abasigne   *Don*

Fred the ~~aborigine~~ was just finished
his walk ~~about it~~. and his wife went with him.
They had finished setting up their house.
~~And~~ Fred ~~he~~ went to bed He woke up
about half an hour later and he heard a noise. He
thinks it's his wife and he said "is that
you.—Honey" and Honey said ~~Help~~ and
Fred ~~got~~ him ~~to~~ setting and had a look
and still heard ~~nothing~~ then he walked
over ~~to~~ the fire and lit up a burning
log and looked around, ~~stomain~~ He saw a
Blacksnake with a gin it ~~stomain~~ Fred said
hommm what a snake. I'm going to have
~~w~~ you for tea and so he killed the snake
and he ate the snake and found his
wife in the snake's stomach and she was still alive
so everything was alright and they said it was
the ~~best~~ snake they had.

FIGURE 1.4

Questions prepared by Don about the picture
1. Why did the snake have a giant stomach?
2. Why did Fred go to bed?
3. Why did the snake eat Fred's wife?

The efforts and materials which the boy has brought to the session became the basis for expansion and development. Each step throughout the session will be given a number indicating the order followed. The steps are as follows:—

1. The therapist says: "Take the words you have made and match them on the appropriate place on the picture and say them as you do so". Here the therapist takes the opportunity to correct any words that are misspelt, such as "brown", taking time to develop some discussion centred around the initial consonant sounds, blends, and other words that contain similar "ow" phonograms. Don is then asked to write down words spoken which have these similarities in them.

2. The therapist observes: "You haven't done many words this week; let's look at the picture and see if we can think of some more 'doing words'. What other words tell us about what the snake does?" Whatever Don replies has to be written down by him. He says: "Wriggling", Therapist, "What else?" D. "Crawling". T. "What's another word?" D. "Hiss". T. "Another?" D. "Slither". T. "Any more?" D. "Strike". The therapist says: "I think we can have some more naming words, also; can you think of any? Look at the picture". He looks over the picture and says "water", "shield", "axe", "noon", and "turtle", which are then written down. The same procedure is followed for the adjectives.

3. As each new word is written, the occasion is taken as a point of departure to teach some simple rule or principle. He had difficulty with the word "turtle" so the "ur" pattern was discussed and the "le" along with other signs making similar sounds. Words with sound and spelling parts similar to "turtle", such as "bottle", "throttle", were considered and written. How to form the past tense was discussed on many previous occasions.

4. The questions which Don had written but had not answered were then considered. He was asked to read his question out aloud, and to give the answer orally, which he was then required to write. He had great difficulty translating into written form what he could sometimes say quite well. The replies to the questions he prepared were as follows:
   1. Because he ate Fred's wife.
   2. He was tired.
   3. Because he was hungry,
all of which he wrote correctly with the exception of the word "because". For this the structured spelling apparatus was used, giving him practice in composing the word, breaking the word and re-composing it against a time limit which he sets himself, with a stopwatch beside him. Other difficult words are handled in this manner.

5.   Next comes a consideration of the story he has written. Don reads the story out aloud with his own copy in front of him. As he does so he sees many errors: words left out, words misspelt and duplication. He pencils in the corrections, takes the story home and brings back a typed or re-written copy next week which he then reads out to the therapist.

     The procedure is repeated weekly with a little additional work of oral reading from a book geared to his interest level.

EVALUATION OF PROGRESS

     After seeing Don for a period of 33 sessions over fourteen months his reading progress was evaluated by the Schonell (1960) Graded Word Test and the Neale Analysis of Reading Ability (1966), and the Daniels and Diack (1960) Standard Reading Test. The results appear in Table 1.3.

TABLE 1.3: Comparing the initial assessment of Don's reading ability with the most recent assessment

Test	Initial assessment	Recent assessment
	13.3.68	*3.6.69*
Schonell Graded Word Test	5 yrs. 7 mths.	8 yrs. 0 mths.
Daniels and Diack Standard Reading Test	6 „ 0 „	8 „ 3 „
Neale Analysis of Reading Ability	not given	7 „ 10 „

     His ability to express himself had also developed remarkably as evidenced by Figure 1.5.

     The boy's whole attitude to life had changed: he now saw hope, and this hope was expressed in many ways, not the least of which being his perception of his future. He saw himself on a self-rating scale as someone who "tried very hard to read", and he had changed his rating from someone who saw his chances of being able to read properly from "hopeless" to "poor". As the therapy sessions concluded he began to talk about a professional career in the army. Therapy was terminated after the forty-eighth session.

     It would be an easy matter to describe Don not only as dyslexic, but also as a case of dysbulia which is defined by English and English (1958) as "difficulty in thinking and giving attention"; but since there is again no satisfactory agreement on the definition, it is better to talk of Don as having chronic reading and spelling disability, linked with a chronic thought-sequencing disability.

CONCLUDING COMMENTS ON THE METHOD

     The method used illustrates an attempt to integrate reading into the total pattern of language structure and development of the child. Each session consists of reading, writing, thinking and organizing the child's responses around a central visual pictorial stimulus with a coherent theme. Such a

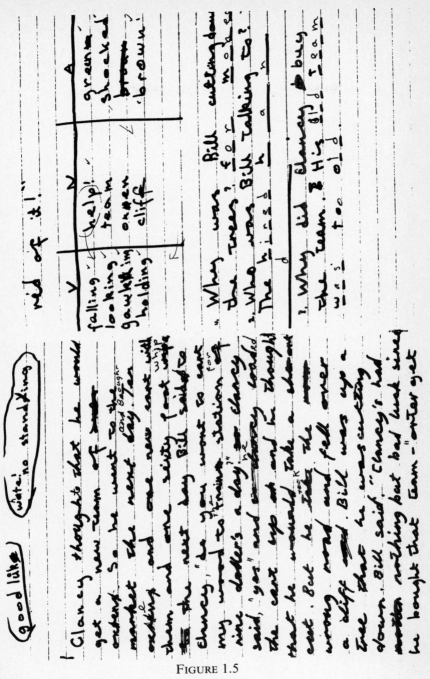

FIGURE 1.5

method provides conceptual focalization within a given framework. It is the task of the therapist to help the child impose structure order and sequence of an abstract kind on the visual representations, which have a degree of concreteness and upon which he focuses. This structure is imposed by an expanding model of more complex hierarchical organization linked with expression, and is illustrated below by a conceptualization in the form of a schematic model.

The central concepts inherent in this approach are that the child begins from a visual field first-order representational level and generates his own concepts, ideas, sequences; that he asks his own questions and answers them. He then has to respond to this self-generated information at three levels:

1.   the oral level,
2.   the written level,
3.   the level of visual decoding (reading).

In such behaviour the child is able both to generate and synchronize all the skills necessary for language and reading development. Thus concept formation, word building and expansion, syntax expression, and finally "read back", are seen as a total process clearly anchored to specific stimulus situations, and not as some experience far removed from the child's world. There is continual self generation feedback and further response.

The approach outlined is merely a stimulus for an integrated approach; it can be applied and extended by the creative and resourceful teacher. It was highly successful for Don and has been equally successful for other disabled children . . . Another life has been salvaged.

REFERENCES

BLOOMFIELD, L. and BARNHART, C. L.: *Let's Read, a Linguistic Approach*. Wayne State University Press, 1963.
BRUNER, J. S.: *Toward a Theory of Instruction*. Belknap Harvard, 1966.
CRITCHLEY, McDonald: *Developmental Dyslexia*. Heinemann, London, 1964.
DANIELS, J. C. and DIACK, H.: *The Standard Reading Tests*. Chatto & Windus, London, 1960.
ENGLISH, H. B. and ENGLISH, A. C.: *A Comprehensive Dictional of Psychological & Psycho-analytical Terms*. Longmans, 1958.
GATTEGNO, C.: *Words in Colour*. Educational Explorers Limited, 1962.
GIBSON, E. J.: Learning to Read *Science*, Vol. 148, May 1965: pp. 1066-1072.
JACKSON, M. S.: The Structured Alphabet. *The Slow Learning Child*, Vol. 16, No. 2, July, 1969.
MONEY, J.: *The Disabled Reader. Education of the Dyslexic Child*, The John Hopkins Press, Baltimore, 1966.
NEALE, M. D.: *Neale Analysis of Reading Ability*. Macmillan, New York, 2nd Edition, 1966.
REID, J. F.: Dyslexia: A Problem of Communication. *Education Research*, Vol. 10, No. 2, February, 1968.
SCHONELL, F. J. and SCHONELL, B. B.: *Diagnostic & Attainment Testing*. Oliver & Boyd, Edinburgh, 1960.

MODEL OF HIERARCHICAL STRUCTURE AND FUNCTIONS INVOLVED IN THE VISUO-THEMATIC APPROACH TO THE TEACHING OF LANGUAGE AND READING TO DON.

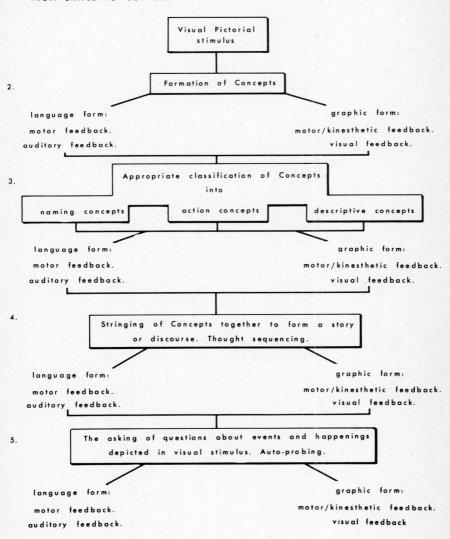

LEVELS OF ABSTRACTION
FROM SIMPLE TO COMPLEX

Visual Pictorial stimulus

2. Formation of Concepts

language form: graphic form:
motor feedback.   motor/kinesthetic feedback.
auditory feedback.   visual feedback.

3. Appropriate classification of Concepts into

naming concepts   action concepts   descriptive concepts

language form: graphic form:
motor feedback.   motor/kinesthetic feedback.
auditory feedback.   visual feedback.

4. Stringing of Concepts together to form a story or discourse. Thought sequencing.

language form: graphic form:
motor feedback.   motor/kinesthetic feedback.
auditory feedback.   visual feedback.

5. The asking of questions about events and happenings depicted in visual stimulus. Auto-probing.

language form: graphic form:
motor feedback.   motor/kinesthetic feedback.
auditory feedback.   visual feedback

Report No. 2

LEARNING TO READ:

A MATTER OF GRASPING

BASIC CONCEPTS

Learning to read: a matter of grasping basic concepts

There is possibly more debate, more discussion, more concern and more categorical statement about the nature of reading than about any other cognitive academic-type activity with which man has concerned himself. It is believed that some 12,000 research reports have been published during the past half century in this area (Levin, 1966). It is said to be more than in any other; yet despite the talk, the research, the almost universal interest, the nature of reading is still obscure.

Annually, about one quarter of the children entering Victorian high schools and technical schools have failed to learn to read appropriately at their expected grade or age level; a small percentage have failed dismally; some one or two per cent are still functioning like Grade 1 and Grade 2 children.

There is a great interest in the concept of remediation: how to treat and remedy the child who has failed, and how to treat the so-called dyslexic child. As more schools do some stocktaking, this need for remediation becomes more apparent. All the emphasis, however, seems to have been on remediation and not on prevention. It is as though the preventative procedures are not known.

Reading disability is a phenomenon known only in the civilised world. It is a by-product of subjecting children to the requirement of responding to sets of squiggles on paper (or in sand, or on rocks, etc.). There is no such thing as a reading disability case amongst the primitive peoples of the world for no such sophisticated demand is made upon them! Even so, in civilized communities it is an unknown phenomenon until the child is confronted with reading stimuli, and that is at about the age of five or six years.

It is soon discovered that some children, without undue effort, make the agreed upon responses to the visual symbols thrust in front of them, while others behave in rather strange ways. Logically, the problem ought to arise when the child first comes to school. Preventative treatment should commence at the infant school level.

Interest in methods of detecting children at risk in reading is mounting. McLeod (1969), for instance, has devised a schedule for predicting dyslexia. Such a procedure is, however, not without some risk as Rosenthal and Jacobson (1968) have shown in their work on the so-called self-fulfilling prophecy. Early detection would be most useful if children at risk could be discovered without such a discovery in any way damaging the child. It is, of course, finally not possible to know whether a child of average intelligence will be a reading disability case until he is confronted with words. Some have argued that it is better to wait until the child has been exposed rather than make a preschool diagnosis. Clearly such a procedure may also have serious implications for the child who fails. Whatever the decision, there are difficulties.

A PREVENTION PROGRAMME

An experimental pilot programme to aid the reading disabled, built around a scientifically designed piece of equipment as its initial and central focus, was conceived. This programme, together with the results of its success on two groups of children, will be reported.

THE ESSENTIALS OF THE PROGRAMME AND PROCEDURE

The apparatus

The entire programme is centred around a piece of equipment known as the structured alphabet kit, previously described briefly by Jackson (1969).

What is the structured alphabet kit?

It is simply a scientifically designed and thoroughly researched piece of equipment to aid the teacher in the beginning reading process, or to aid the disabled reader.

The kit is a box 17 inches long, with 27 compartments each large enough to house a bank of five copies of each of the 27 currently used English graphemic shapes (or letters). (See Figure 2.1.)

Each of the letter shapes are on tablets approximately one quarter of an inch thick. These stand together vertically in their respective compartments, with the letter signs facing the pupil. The letter tablets are easily removed, since they stand three eighths of an inch above the top of the container when the lid is opened, exposing the contents. The container is built on a base sufficiently wide for the child to be able to assemble both letters, words and sentences. This base has a ledge and contains 7 housing slots which will variously take three letter words, four letter words or five letter words respectively. The entire kit is very light and is designed to sit on a desk or table in front of the child.

A number of principles have been built into the kit. These centre around five broad divisions:

1. *Those relating to the accessibility of letter signs.*
    Here, three aspects were taken into account.
    (a) Compartmentalization: twenty-seven compartments are built into the kit so that each of the letters may be housed without confusion in

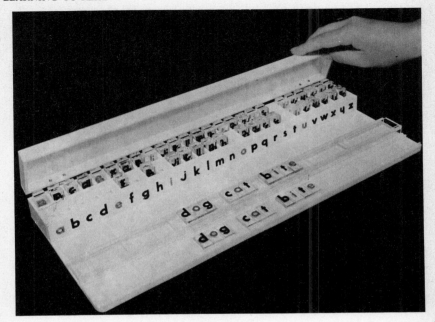

FIGURE 2.1

an identifiable slot and located with minimum effort, thus unconsciously teaching the so-called a, b, c. A further reason for this design
was to aid in giving letters identity in their own right as shapes and
entities, though it is, of course, recognised that they have real meaning
only when they occupy a place in a word.

(b) On the front of each compartment the letter sign to be housed
therein is displayed. This means that letters may be replaced in their
respective locations by a simple process of matching letter to letter.

(c) The compartments were identified with the usual alphabetic signs
on the outside in the order of a to z. This was done to facilitate famili-
arity with this sequential order so that generalization to dictionary and
cataloguing skills could be readily facilitated.

2. *Those relating to the structure and nature of the letter signs and tablets.*
    (a) A distinction was made in the colour coding between the five
    graphemic representations of the vowels and consonants most regularly
    recognized in English. The vowel signs are red and the consonant signs
    are black, in order to demonstrate, and thus facilitate the under-
    standing of the basic notion that words are composed of both vowels
    and consonants.

    (b) A distinguishing code in the form of a line is engraved on the
    bottom of each of the tablets to facilitate the rapid recognition of top
    and bottom, thus preventing signs being viewed upside down.

(c) Each of the letter signs is embossed or raised above its background; thus the sign appears in a three dimensional sense. This was done to diminish confusion between figure and ground—the letter sign being figure and the tablet on which it was placed, ground.

(d) The letter tablets are made one quarter of an inch thick to facilitate handling by young children and those with minor motor disabilities.

(e) Five copies of each letter sign were made to be housed in the form of a letter bank within each compartment, so that a number of words or even short sentences may be made without replacement of letters being necessary.

3. *Those relating to the use and handling of the kit.*

(a) The container is supported on a base which extends to the front towards the user. On this base containing a small ledge and slots, there is ample room to manipulate the letter tablets and to make words or sentences as the case may be. At the front edge of the base are a series of container slots for housing three, four and five letter words. This was done to assist the child's eye to remain contained within the slot boundaries, thus focussing on the word constructed and its parameters.

(b) The kits were designed to sit on a desk in front of the user for ready access. They may be used in an individual setting, with an adult present, guiding the learning process, or in a group setting of up to

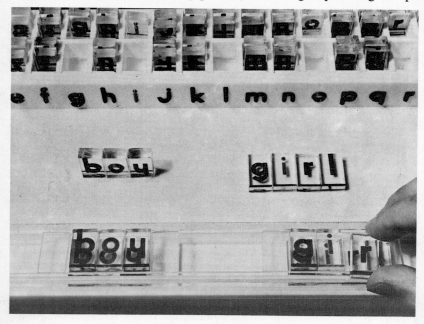

FIGURE 2.2

eight pupils. The maximum number of pupils recommended for ideal use in a group setting, however, is considered to be about four.

4.   *That relating to a special and pre-reading or remedial device.*

Attached to the front of the base of the kit is a special device to facilitate the procedure of matching. (See Figure 2.2).

A very experienced principal of the infant department of a school has reported that apart from the advantage mentioned, children can "make" and "break" words long before they can write, and this has two major advantages at the beginning reading stage:

(a)   Errors are not stamped in through the motor system, and

(b)   the child is able to cope with this task immediately.

She has further said that when working with a group of children one can more easily see the errors children make by watching where their hands go to select letters to compose words, and because of the colour coding of vowels and consonants.

5.   The final consideration, and an important one for the busy teacher, is that of storage. The letter tablets are securely housed in the box with a hinged wooden lid, thus preventing tablets being spilled and facilitating storage in the form of stacking. Many of the principles just described may be seen by viewing Figure 2.1.

THE TEACHING PRINCIPLES AND PROCEDURE

The uses of the kit in facilitating pre-reading—a revolutionary proposal

At this point it must be stressed that the kit is intended both as an aid (a) to help children in the beginning stages of reading, and (b) as an aid in solving the dilemmas of the child who has failed to read. It may be used in conjunction with an already established and ongoing programme or as part of an initial programme as is being done with non-English speaking migrant children who have just arrived in Australia.

One of the questions that bedevils the teaching of beginning reading is how to prepare the child for the task. This preparatory task is generally referred to as reading readiness and receives a place in almost every text-book on reading (see Dechant, 1964, for example).

There have been numerous long-established practices mostly centred around the phenomena of matching and classifying similar and different objects, pictures or shapes.

In more recent years there has been a vigorous growth of visual perceptual type activities epitomized in programmes such as the Frostig (1964) programme for visual perception.

The kit is constructed with a built-in device enabling the revolutionary pre-reading and remedial activity of superimposed matching, thus virtually eliminating forever the possibility of incorrect matching as a first step in visual perceptual reading type activities. Most pre-reading activities and programmes are built on the assumption that an involvement in the kinds of activities which they recommend will aid the behaviour of reading. The assumption is based on the concept of generalization which has been thoroughly researched and occupies a distinguished place in any textbook on learning. However, a scrutiny of the activities suggested shows that they are so far removed from what reading behaviour looks like that any relationship they might conceivably have to such a phenomenon would be entirely fortuitous. Recently an experienced teacher of retarded children remarked that there were some children at the end of six years in a special school who were absolutely expert at the pre-reading exercises given but could still hardly read a word!

If we want to prepare children for reading, we should move operationally close to the dependent variable of reading behaviour. The pre-reading stage may be conceptualized as involving the concepts and symbols which the child will later use. Instead of matching circles to circles, squares to squares and so on, all of which may be very interesting, the child should be brought immediately to the task of matching letters to letters and words to words.

THE METHOD OF SUPERIMPOSED MATCHING

Usually in any matching exercise the child is required to match or classify one set of objects with another set, both in the horizontal plane and in a juxtaposed position. That is, a child might be asked to match all of one kind with all of another kind and he is required to select those which match and put them beside the others. This matching procedure is often very difficult for some young children as their eyes have to move from the objects, say on the left hand side, to those on the right hand side, or to draw a line from those on one side to those on the other.

The method of superimposition absolutely eliminates this problem. The teacher places the model in the appropriate module at the front of the structured alphabet kit and places the clear cover screen, similarly moduled as the base, over the top. The child is then required to match, in a superimposed fashion, his example to the model under the clear plastic cover. The modular slot both on the base and cover means that the letter tablets cannot easily move during the matching. They hold the subjects' efforts secure upon completion (see Figure 2.2.).

The procedure has been used with a severely retarded five year old boy who after twenty one-hour sessions could attend a normal state school, and who was able after three months at school to read his first preparatory reader in the Happy Venture series.

METHOD USED WITH A GROUP OF RETARDED READERS

The following procedure, to be described, was used with a group of slow learner Grade II children on a daily half hourly basis throughout the year.[2] The teacher had a kit three times the size of the one just described (see Figure 2.3).

[2]The degree of weakness of the pupils may be seen by reference to the research report at the end of this discussion.

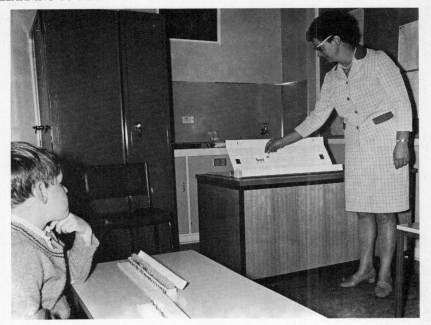

FIGURE 2.3

In the discussion which follows, some of the concepts thought to be essential for an effective grasp of reading by beginning readers will be discussed. The discussion will focus on ways in which the apparatus may be used to aid the acquisition of concepts.

1. *The concept of letter differences and matching practice*

The child is told that this is a box containing lots of different kinds of signs or letters. He is then given plenty of visual discrimination and matching practice; that is, he takes out two different groups of letters: all of the "b" tablets and all of the "a" tablets, for example. He places each lot in a different rubber ring provided for the purpose. He is then instructed to put them back in their respective compartments. (Each of the compartments has the letter sign on the outside for identification purposes.) The first few sessions consist entirely of this kind of matching practice beginning initially with either the vowels or the consonants, or both, depending on the teacher's preference. No mention is made at this stage of the concept of vowels and consonants, or of sounds or names. It is important, however, to avoid the combined use of consonant signs involving mirror images or reversals such as, b, d, u, n, p, q and the like in the initial sessions.

2. *The concept that letters have tops and bottoms or a right and wrong way up*

Each of the letter signs is engraved on a tablet with the bottom clearly marked by a fine red or black line underneath the sign. The children are given a lot of practice; a pile of letter tablets is placed on the table and they are asked to put them the right way up. The teacher points out that the red or black line is at the bottom and enters into a discussion with the children about the concepts "top" and "bottom".

Because a letter tablet is about a quarter of an inch thick, it is possible to stand it up vertically with the line indicating bottom, actually at the bottom! (See Figure 2.2.) After this is well established, the child is shown how to place the tablets in the horizontal plane, by placing the bottom near the ledge on the base.

3. *The concept of vowels and consonants*

The child is now told that there are two sets of letters in this box.

(a) One set is called the vowel set and they are coloured red. The teacher shows the child some samples, encourages him to say what they are called and to take them out and replace them. He is given a red rubber ring in which to place members of the vowel set.

(b) The second set of letters are called consonants. They are coloured black. The teacher shows the child some samples, which he takes out and replaces. The child is then given a black rubber ring in which to place members of the consonant set.

Although the distinction between vowels and consonants should be frequently and often referred to, it should not be laboured. The child is now given a lot of practice discriminating between vowels and consonants by simply responding to the instruction "put some vowels inside the red rubber ring", or "put some consonants inside the black rubber ring". Pointing to a vowel sign, the teacher asks him to name what set, family or group it belongs to. Similarly, with signs belonging to the "consonant" set, family or group.

Relevant practice such as this is intended to establish the basic visual discrimination of the major letter groupings and thereby aid in the subsequent auditory and visual discrimination of vowel and consonant signs.

4. *The concept that signs stand for sounds*

This step involves communicating the idea that signs stand for sounds. The teacher says: "when we say the sound 'p' we write it or make it like this". Here the teacher selects a consonant and its representative signs, for example, the letter tablet with the sign "p" on it. The teacher asks the children to "select" the same one from their box, make the sound orally in response to it, feel its shape and put it away. This kinesthetic experience with letters can be best gained by placing the letters or words in the word-housing modules at the front of the kit. The child is blindfolded and asked to feel the letter or word which cannot move about because they are securely held the correct way up. Young disabled readers who have never had such an experience found it most rewarding to sort out one letter from another, and one word from another. This procedure is then repeated till fluency is reached. As soon as fluency is reached the instructor produces a "whole" word, such as "pot", and simultaneously the tablets containing the appropriate signs, assembles them and shows that we now have a word. Thus by selecting "p", "o" and "t", and teaching the sounds of these three signs, the first word is read. Representative pictures or objects along with the whole word may be shown to reinforce the concept of a word. The child may now "break" and remake this word at will. This idea that arrangement and re-arrangement is critical for signalling word meaning is reinforced and clarified by re-arranging the letter signs to make the word "top". The child is instructed to listen carefully to the difference. Alteration of the initial and final consonant will make this idea more apparent. Gradually and slowly more vowels and consonants are introduced, *embedding them in words as this is done.* Contrastive exercises suggested by linguists such as Fries (1963) may now be introduced. Examples are as follows: "cat, hat"; "pin, pan"; "mat, map". The child is asked which one is different or which one is the same. He is invited to hold the final vowel and consonant segment constant and alter the initial consonant to signal a different word.

The idea that certain sound signs combine or cluster to produce a single sound should be introduced. Those consonant sounds common to the initial position are:

th	st	wh	sh	br	ch	dr	tr	cl
fr	gr	pl	sm	tw	gl	sw	sp	

Those common to the final position are:

sh	ch	al	on	ck	ty	nk
lk	by	nt	rk	se	ly	

In addition, phonograms, which are those end spelling patterns in English which have a fairly stable sound-sign relationship, should be introduced. Those with high frequency at the Grade 1 and 2 level (after Durrell, 1956) are:

Grade 1:

in	and	ike	ake	oke	ook	own	ed	oy
ay	as	ig	ouse	at	an	un	am	it
ome	ack	ank	ut	un	ell	all	ill	ame
og	ee	up	id	ool	en	oll	ot	op
ap	ing	on						

Grade 2:

ue	eet	ive	oom	op	oot	unk	ight	eep
ich	ore	ent	oss	uy	ilk	ead	ease	om
ass	eat	ith	orse	out	arn	ird	ern	our
eak	ink	alk	arm	one	ora	ilk	ile	old
aid	int	ood	eet					

Grade 3:

ouk	een	ought	igh	tion	atch	itch	ob
ix	eel	eek	ush	tch	eech	orn	eal
oast	ound	ut	ough	age	oil	ure	

As well as this, prefixes and suffixes should be introduced as follows:

Suffixes Grade 1:

s . os . ed . ing . y .

Prefixes and Suffixes Grade 2:

   Prefixes

   con   ex   in   en   el   up   de

   Suffixes

   ly   ty   er   est   ion

Prefixes and Suffixes Grade 3:

   Prefixes

   re   di   bi   be   per   any   un   for   el

   Suffixes

   ily   ier   iest   ant   ous   ious   out

5. *The concept that letters or signs which stand for sounds can combine
    to make words*

In an extension of the previous notion, the child is invited to listen to
the difference between single type sounds (phonetics) which are represented
by single type letters (graphemes) and combinations of sounds into words
(morphemes). The phoneme "o" and the morpheme "pot" may be used
to illustrate this point.

He is taken from the sounds and shown their graphemic representations
and told "We can take the consonant 'p' and 't', put them in the 'consonant ring' and put the vowel in the 'vowel ring'. Now watch while we
show you how to make a word. This is how we do it".

"We'll take the sign 'p' first (always using the sound for 'p' and not its
name at this stage), then the letters 'o' then 't'. Now by putting all the signs
together in a special way (teacher demonstrates by assembling the word
with the letters in a left to right fashion) we have a little word 'pot' and it is
made up of the sounds 'p', 'o', 't', (listen) and the signs 'p', 'o', 't', (look),
and feel (touch the raised signs)".

The child is then given practice in making and breaking the word and
reassembling it from the jumbled letters.

The next step is to tell him that if we change the letters about and the sounds (listen) we can make a different kind of word. "Let's try putting 't' first, then 'o', then 'p'. Now we have the word top (t-op)".

The child is then given a lot of practice at making simple words of this kind in response to oral instructions given by the teacher, where he listens carefully to the sounds and makes the words from the sounds he has mastered. The simple words may be nonsense words such as "pog", "gop", "op", "ot", "tog", provided they represent a one to one sound-sign relationship and represent the sounds heard in English. A child should not be confronted with nonsense words which have graphemic representations that are unlawful, e.g., "gieg".

The concept "first" was used in this discussion. The instruction to the children was: "Let's put the sign 'p' out first and next to it put the letter for 'o' and at the end, or next, put the letter for 't' ". Each of these concepts, first, next and end, has to be taught. It was found necessary to teach the concept "first" or "beginning" by using markers such as little "green" tablets. The display rack at the front of the kit was divided into modular slots, some capable of holding only three letter words and so on up to five letter words. Thus it was possible then to assemble the word, beginning at the green markers and placing the remaining number of letters in the modular slot. It was observed that when children were instructed to put out the sign for the sounds "p" and then the sign for the sound "o" after it, the concept "after it" had no meaning; sometimes it was put on the left-hand side of the "p" and sometimes on the right-hand side. This difficulty of visual sequencing was, however, overcome by the use of the markers and the housing slots.

6. *The concept of patterns and codes, by use of vowels and consonants in various arrangements*

Linguists have distinguished various vowel and consonant combinations which have been described by Lamb (1967) as spelling patterns. They are, of course, also reading patterns in the beginning stages of reading.

In order to facilitate learning and firmly embed these stable patterns, a pattern keyboard was given to each of the children (Figure 2.4).

There are four patterns—

(i) C.V.C. (consonant-vowel-consonant) is the first, and this is the simplest and most stable pattern of English spelling and reading. The children were given ample practice in simply selecting a consonant, a vowel, a consonant, and placing them in that order on the pattern key boards. They were then asked to see if they could guess their words and make new ones by altering the initial and final consonants. Thus—

(a) changing the initial consonants

bad	sad	had	pad
bed	red	fed	ned
ran	pan	fan	can

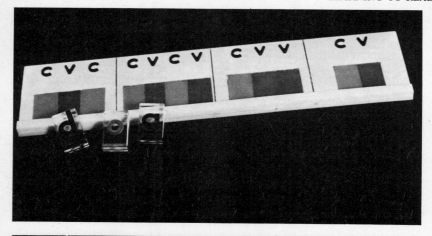

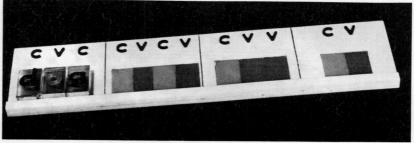

FIGURE 2.4

At a later stage consonant clusters or blends are introduced and treated similarly—

*b*ad	*s*ad	*g*lad
*b*ed	*r*ed	*s*led
*r*an	*f*an	*c*lan

(b) changing the final consonants

pa*n*	pa*d*	pa*t*
co*t*	co*d*	co*p*

and later final consonant clusters

ba*n*	ban*d*	ban*k*

(c) substituting for the given vowel in this pattern—

p*a*t	p*e*t	p*i*t	p*o*t
d*i*g	d*o*g	d*u*g	d*a*g
s*i*n	s*a*n	s*o*n	s*u*n

The following rules applicable to the C.V.C. pattern taken from Burmeister (1968) will be found useful at this stage, and will provide the intelligent reader who is prone to making visual perceptual errors with an alternative means of breaking the code.

(a) If the only vowel letter is at the end of a word, the letter usually stands for a long sound (one-syllable words only). (be, he, she, go)
(b) When "consonant + y" are the final letters in a one syllable word, the "y" has a "long i" sound; in a polysyllabic word the "y" has a "short i" (long e) sound. (my, by, cry; baby, dignity)
(c) A single vowel in a closed syllable has a short sound, except that it may be modified in words in which the vowel is followed by an "r". (club, dress, at, car, pumpkin, virgin)
(d) The "r" gives the preceding vowel a sound that is neither long nor short (car, care, far, fair, fare). (single or double vowels)

Two forms of dictation are stressed at this stage of acquisition—
(a) visual dictation. The teacher displays the word on her display board, then the child does so on his; she then says the word after the children have made their words and checks for correctness.
(b) oral dictation. The teacher says the words and the child makes his imitation of what she has said from his letter tablets. She then presents her model visually, saying it again very carefully. The children then proceed to make a visual check listening to the auditory components as they do so. The child, having made his model and having had it checked for correctness, is then instructed to "break" it and remake the model from the letter components.
(ii) Pattern 2 consists of a consonant-vowel-consonant and final vowel, thus: C.V.C. + e. This pattern usually instructs the reader that the final "e" is silent and the preceding vowel says its own name. This pattern is not introduced till the preceding one is thoroughly mastered. By this stage, however, the child will be able to respond verbally to (i.e., read) simple words like at, cat, bat, sat, etc., and by giving him examples, as follows, he will master the idea.

a+	+	e	ate
rob	"	"	robe
kit	"	"	kite'
hat	"	"	hate
mat	"	"	mate

He is asked to make simple words from the letter tablets and, as the teacher instructs him, to add an "e". He is then asked what this does to the word and it is expected that after practice he will understand this well. The teacher then proceeds to give oral and visual dictation and the child responds by making words with the letters. He then moves on to more difficult words such as save, gave, home, came, hive, dive, drive, like, bike, etc. The rule may be stated that when a word ends in a "vowel-consonant-e" pattern, the "e" is silent, but the preceding vowel may be long or short, such as in cape, mile, have, late, line, come, prove. Although this pattern or rule has many exceptions it holds good for about 66 per cent of English words.
(iii) Pattern 3 consists of a consonant-vowel-vowel-consonant (C.V.V.C.), such as in train, rain, leaf, feed, coat, goat, need, seed. There are three

useful generalizations which may be taught to children here (Burmeister, 1968).

(a) Digraphs: When the following double vowel combinations are seen together the first is usually long and the second silent: ai as in pay, day ay, as in main, train; ca as in cat; ea may also have a short "e" sound as in bread, dead, head; ee as in see, oa as in oat, ou as bow, now ow also has an "ou" sound as in howl, cow.

The double vowels or digraphs for which generalizations are not possible are au, ou, ui, and eu. However, "aw" and "oy" have a reasonable degree of consistency and can be taught as "aw" in shaw and "oy" as in boy.

(b) The dipthongs or blends: the following double vowel combinations usually blend—

au auto, ou house, oi coin, oy boy, ook book, rooster.

Further, "id" and "ia" after "c", "t", or "s" help to make a consonant sound as in vicious, partial, musician, vision and attention.

(iv) Pattern 4 consists of a C.V. pattern such as in be, me, he, go, so, no. Double vowel endings come within this category (e.g., day, say and bee).

IMPORTANCE OF RULES

Since it is often felt that rules are a burden, some explanation of their function may be in order. The importance of rules as clues needs to be stressed. A rule is simply a functional device, a cognitive map, for enabling a child who comes to a difficult decision to fall back on a strategy which helps him make the one most appropriate. This is illustrated by a child being confronted in reading with an unfamiliar word beginning with c, for example, the word "certain". He is faced with a simple decision: will he pronounce the "cert" as "ker" or will he pronounce it as "ser"? The rule which says: " 'c' followed by 'e', 'i', or 'y' sounds soft like 's', otherwise 'c' is hard like 'k' " should help him decide. The diagram below presents the function of rules in a schematic fashion.

THE FUNCTION OF RULES SCHEMATICALLY PRESENTED

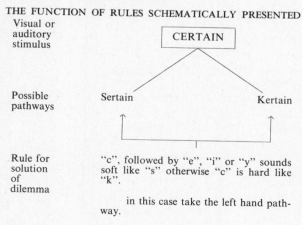

Visual or auditory stimulus

CERTAIN

Possible pathways   Sertain   Kertain

Rule for solution of dilemma

"c", followed by "e", "i" or "y" sounds soft like "s" otherwise "c" is hard like "k".

in this case take the left hand pathway.

The following rules about consonant sounds should be borne in mind and taught as the occasion demands.

(a) "C" followed by "e", "i", or "y" sounds soft; otherwise "c" is hard (omit "ch"). (certain, city, cycle; attic, cat, clip, success)

(b) "G" followed by "e", "i" or "y" sounds soft; otherwise "g" is hard (omit "gh"). (gell, agile, gypsy; gone, flag, grope; suggest)

(c) "Ch" is usually pronounced as it is in "kitchen", not like "sh" as in "machine".

(d) When a word ends in "ck", it has the same last sound as in "look".

(e) When "ght" is seen in a word, "gh" is silent. (thought, night, right)

(f) When two of the same consonants are side by side, only one is heard. (dollar, paddle)

RESEARCH REPORT NO. 1 A PILOT PROJECT

This is a report on a pilot project in an infant department of a state school where children had already failed in their efforts to learn to read. A preventative remediation programme was designed and carried out over a 12-month period. The results reported here constitute an evaluation after the programme had been in progress for that time. The remedial programme was carried out in a group setting with eight children seated around tables in a hollow square (see Figures 2.5 and 2.6).

FIGURE 2.5

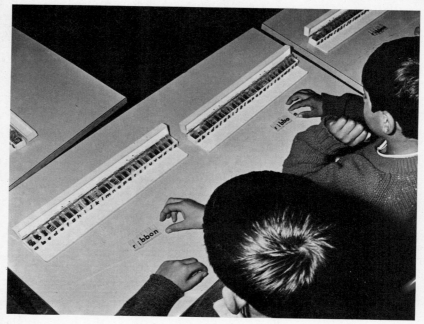

FIGURE 2.6

The Sample

An experimental and control group procedure was used. The experimental group had come to Grade 2 and had been diagnosed as having failed to make satisfactory progress by the class teacher. Their mean reading age on the Daniels and Diack Standard Reading Test (1958) immediately prior to the commencement of treatment was 5.5 years. Their average chronological age was 6.6, therefore they were functioning on the average at a reading level 12 months below that of their C.A., a severe state of retardation to have in their early school career.

In order to avoid the criticism that a known control group might also unconsciously receive favourable treatment, the procedure adopted here was to choose a post-treatment group who had a mean IQ significantly higher than the experimental group in order to test the power of the procedure. It was argued that rather than selecting two equal groups, treating one as experimental and the other as a control, the procedure of attempting to compare a retarded group with a higher IQ group would be more appropriate. This was achieved by taking a group of children from a neighbouring state school. The mean IQ of this control group was 16 points higher than the experimental group.[3] They had been to school for the same length of time as the experimental group, and were being taught by a competent teacher who gave extra help to these pupils who were regarded as a little weak but "certainly not in need of remedial assistance". No actual pretest of their reading ability was made so as not to draw attention to the fact that the group would be used in the way intended, thus avoiding a Hawthorn effect.

TABLE 2.1: Summary of characteristics of the sample

	Pre-Test		Post-Test	
	Exp. Group (6 males; 2 females)	Cont. Group (6 males; 2 females)	Exp. Group (6 males; 2 females)	Cont. Group (6 males; 2 females)
C.A.	6.6	6.6	7.65	7.62
S.D.	0.46	0.22	0.46	0.22
Reading Age	5.5	—	6.81	6.87
S.D.			0.37	0.87
IQ (WISC)	75.62	92.25	—	—

^{3}t = 4.77 (t test for independent samples)
p = .005.

The Results

All of the eight reading disabled children, who were also well below average in intelligence, after receiving educational therapy along the lines discussed, increased considerably in their reading ability at the end of the 12-month period. The average increase was in fact 13.4 months, which is a rate of gain that might be predicted for better than average children. Considering that the average IQ of the children of the group was 75, the progress must be considered rather remarkable. The individual improvements are set out in Table 2.2 below. It will be noted by observing the table that the lowest gain was 9 months and the highest gain was 19 months.

TABLE 2.2: The gains in reading age scores on the Daniels and Diack Standard .Reading Test made by the experimental group of low IQ children after 12 months of educational therapy

Subjects	Age 1st Feb. 1970	Reading Age Test 1	Reading Age Test 2	Reading Score: gain in months	Reading Standard	
					1st Test	2nd Test
1.	8.1	5.7	6.5	10	2	3
2.	7.2	5.6	6.7	13	1	4
3.	6.10	5.8	6.5	9	2	3
4.	6.11	5.9	6.9	12	2	4
5.	7.1	6.1	7.7	18	3	5
6.	7.4	5.3	6.7	16	0	4
7.	6.10	5.6	6.5	11	1	3
8.	6.3	5.5	7.0	19	1	4

It will be seen that in three instances the reading ages at the end of the 12 months' treatment exceeded that of the chronological age.

When compared with the control group whose mean IQ was 16.83 points higher, there was precisely no difference in their reading skills and less variation in their scores. Table 2.3 summarizes this data.

TABLE 2.3: A comparison of the mean reading age on the Daniels and Diack Standard Reading Test in the experimental and control groups at the end of 12 months' educational therapy

	Experimental Group	Control Group
Mean Reading Age	6.81	6.87
Standard Deviation	0.37	0.87

Conclusion

These results would appear to indicate that the methodological procedure outlined is of use when attempting to help the disabled reader. It is assumed that the success came about mainly from the use of the structured alphabet kit with its built-in controls. These controls enabled the child to come to terms with the orthographic stimuli in a consistently structured way around a set of comprehensible concepts. It is further assumed that the fact that each child had his own set of equipment which gave a sense of reality and "thingness" to the operation of reading, was of major importance to the disabled reader.

All of the children expressed delight with the daily half-hour sessions and eagerly looked forward to the encounter with reading. This high level of motivation provided by the equipment and the way in which it was handled by the teacher made learning to read a pleasure for a group of children otherwise doomed to failure and a miserable life at school.

RESEARCH REPORT NO. 2 ON THE PREVENTION OF CHRONIC READING DISABILITY IN MIGRANT CHILDREN

Non-speaking English migrant children coming to Australia are not given specialized reading programs but are placed in the normal classroom and expected to cope. Some do cope, but others become hopelessly lost under the double burden of adjustment: to a new society and a new language. This is a report of a study conducted in one school where migrant children are sent, upon arrival in Australia.

The Sample

Two groups of beginners upon arrival at the school were assigned respectively to an experimental group with a mean age of 7.4 and a control group with a mean age of 7.6. Since they did not speak any English no pretests were given of any kind. The basis of assignment into the two groups was purely random.

The experimental group comprised 8 children as there were only eight sets of experimental apparatus and a similar number were in the control group. The experimental group was treated according to the principles set out in the preliminary section of this study. Two weeks before the treatment concluded two children left the school from both the control and experimental groups to locations where their parents had found permanent accommodation.

Each group was given a total of forty 30-40 minute sessions of treatment daily. The experimental group took two sessions or approximately one hour to identify all the letter sounds using the apparatus. It became clear that their ability to 'sound' words, blend sounds and identify words far outstripped their ability to absorb and recall meaning, hence a good part of each session was spent attempting to communicate meaning.

The Results

After four months of treatment their progress in reading was evaluated using the Daniels and Diack Standard Reading Tests. The mean reading age of the control group was found to be 5-6 years and that of the experimental group 6.3 years. The mean difference between the two groups in their reading ability was thus nine months after four months at school. More importantly however they scored highly on the beginning and end consonantal blends as well as the polysyllabic words of the Daniels and Diack test. On the 'beginning' consonantal blends test, the mean number of errors of the control group was 15.3 and that of the experimental group 2.4. Similarly on the 'end' consonantal blends test, the mean number of errors of the control group was 12.1 and of the experimental group 2.1. The mean number of errors difference between the two groups on the polysyllabic words test was 7. The first of these differences was statistically very significant and the others approaching significance—see Table 2.4 for these results.

TABLE 2.4: The results of the experimental and control group of migrant children on four of the Daniels and Diack Standard Reading Tests after 4 months' treatment

Control group $\bar{X}$ age = 7.6				Experimental group $\bar{X}$ age = 7.4			
Reading Age	Consonantal blends begin : end		Poly-syllabic words test	Reading Age	Consonantal blends begin : end		Poly-syllabic words test
5.8	16	2	7	7.0	0	0	0
5.2	22	16	15	6.1	4	0	5
6.3	9	7	5	5.9	0	2	6
5.8	6	8	10	6.7	1	0	0
5.6	18	6	15	5.6	9	6	14
5.2	22	16	15	6.5	2	5	1
	$\bar{X}$ = 15.3	$\bar{X}$ = 12.1	$\bar{X}$ = 11.1		$\bar{X}$ = 2.4	$\bar{X}$ = 2.1	$\bar{X}$ = 4.2

Two of the children were identical twins. The child in the experimental group had a reading age 2 months in advance of his twin.

In addition to this younger group of children an older experimental and control group of 6 children respectively whose mean ages were respectively 10 years and 10.4 years were given 13 hours of treatment as a group, spread over 6 weeks. In the test at the end of the 6 weeks of treatment, the experimental group had a reading age 13 months in advance of their control counterparts. They also showed a marked superiority over the control group on the consonantal blends and polysyllabic words. This difference however was not as great as the difference found in the younger groups.

Conclusion

Considering the rapid progress made by both the younger and the older groups, it would appear to be of crucial significance to migrant children that they be given strategies for coping with the reading of their 'foreign' language at the earliest opportunity. It would not seem to be a disadvantage that the ability to recognize words had outstripped their ability to cope with meaning. The most logical approach to the teaching of reading and language to foreign-speaking migrant children would appear to be that of simultaneous presentation of reading and language stimuli. In this way they gain a rapid grasp of both tasks necessary for their feelings of success and well-being in a new community. This treatment procedure has important preventative and adjustment implications. If we are going to continue to bring migrant children to Australia they should be given every opportunity to cope with the initial language and reading task with the least possible frustration. Prevention is better than cure.

The older group of children were so exited about their success that they repeatedly asked the teacher when they could have their next session.

REFERENCES

BURMEISTER, L. E.: Usefulness of Phonic Generalizations. *The Reading Teacher*, Vol. 21, No. 4, p. 349, Jan, 1968.
DANIELS, J. C. and DIACK, H.: *The Standard Reading Tests*. Chatto and Windus, London, 1958.
DECHANT, E. V.: *Improving the Teaching of Reading*. Prentice Hall, 1964.
DURRELL, D. DeW.: *Improving Reading Instruction*. Harcourt Brace, 1956.
FRIES, C. C.: *Linguistics and Reading*. Holt, Rinehart and Winston, New York, 1963.
FROSTIG, M. and HORNE, D.: *The Frostig Program for the Development of Visual Perception*. Follett Publishing Co., Chicago, 1964.
JACKSON, M. S.: The Structured Alphabet. *Slow Learning Child*, Vol. 16, No. 2, July 1969, pp. 112-117.
LAMB, P.: *Linguistics in Proper Perspective*. C. E. Merrill, Columbus, Ohio, 1967.
LEVIN, H.: The Psychology of Reading, pp. 154-164, in Bruner, J. (ed.). *Learning about Learning*. U.S. Department of Health, Education and Welfare, Office of Education, Washington, 1966.
McLEOD, J.: *Handbook for Dyslexia Schedule and School Entrance Check List*. University of Queensland Press, Brisbane, 1969.
ROSENTHAL, R. and JACOBSON, L. F.: Teacher Expectations for the Disadvantaged. *Scientific American*, Vol. 218, No. 4, April, 1968.

Report No. 3

FROM THE WORLD OF

MENTAL DEFICIENCY TO

THE LIGHT OF A

NORMAL SCHOOL

From the world of mental deficiency to the light of a normal school

This is a report of a boy who had been placed in a day training centre essentially on two criteria. He tested low on an IQ test but this result was not low enough to place him in a day training centre; secondly his behaviour was so aggressive and hyperactive that he could not have been tolerated elsewhere.

EARLY HISTORY

Carl was born on 2 July, 1965. The birth was apparently normal and the prenatal history without any event that could be considered in any way to be unusual or abnormal.

His early physical developmental patterns were not exceptional although he did not walk till 18 months which was perhaps a little later than the average child. By 22 months he had achieved bowel control and by 42 months he had attained bladder control.

His language development was very retarded and at 48 months he could only attempt to say some half dozen words or so and these attempts were very poor indeed and hard to comprehend. His mother reported however that he seemed to understand everything she said. Later actual checks were made on his ability to carry out instructions, and he appeared to be able both to understand and obey.

Up till the age of four his mother observed that he always seemed to be knocking his head. One of the most disturbing features of his development however was his extreme hyperactivity, aggressiveness and hostility. His mother regarded him as a "terrible menace". He would throw violent tantrums, throwing plates, toys and objects about the house, kick the furniture, kick and bite his parents, and knock other children about. This disturbing behaviour and his inability to speak led the mother to seek help. A short account of her attempts to find a solution follow.

At fourteen months he was placed on the drug Stelezine. At three years of age his hearing was checked by a specialist who confirmed that there was no abnormality. The mother's next move was to take him to a psychiatrist who assessed him at 3 years of age as of "average" intelligence. The mother was not at all convinced that a boy who could not speak, and who was a behavioural monster could be average, so she then had him further assessed by a psychologist whose diagnosis placed him in the mentally retarded category (IQ 64—on the Stanford Binet). The mother made an attempt to have him placed in a normal kindergarten but his behaviour. was so disruptive that he was not permitted to stay. Finally he was admitted to a day training centre for the trainable mentally retarded. For this placement he was again seen by another psychologist who confirmed the earlier diagnosis of mental retardation. His mother was desperate to get help for her child and after many enquiries she discovered that Monash University was interested in children's problems. He was duly admitted to the Child Study Centre at Monash in December, 1969 where additional evidence of his intelligence was obtained from the Harris-Goodenough Draw A Man test. His drawing may be seen by reference to Figure 3.1 which indicated a level of intelligence similar to that obtained on the Binet.

An attempt was made to give him the Illinois Test of Psycholinguistics. Owing to his hyperactivity, aggressiveness and inability to speak it was possible to obtain scores on only four of the sub-tests. These are shown in Table 3.1. It will be seen that his auditory reception score was low, but this may have been due to his inattentiveness and hyperactivity. The visual memory and closure scores were also low.

FIGURE 3.1

TABLE 3.1: Carl's scores on the Illinois Test of Psycholinguistics

Auditory Reception	2.2
Visual Reception	4.10
Visual Memory	3.4
Visual Closure	3.6

His aggressiveness may be further illustrated by an extract from the therapist's notes taken on the subject's behaviour after he had been in therapy for four sessions:

"He knocked all the puzzles off the table after the presentation. I made him pick them up to the count of three. He is kicking me under the table. I ignore it. He has again knocked everything on the ground on the fourth presentation. I gave him three to pick them up. He 'splurted' his tongue out at me.

He snatched my pencil and made an aggressive gesture at the apparatus. He continues to make faces and poke his tongue out and is calling out "bah" when poking out his tongue"; and again

"He slapped me on the hand and put his feet on the table. He covered his mouth with a severe clench and kicked the table. He then wiped part of the apparatus off the table again. He had to be forcibly restrained from running away."

Four sessions later:

"He is still very aggressive and kicks the apparatus off the table with his feet! He makes loud "bah" sounds."

After three months he was becoming co-operative; the notes read:

"The subject now always wants to pack up the puzzles so I ask him to hold the object and 'tip' the words into my hand."

THE NATURE OF THE PROBLEM

Four problems required urgent attention—

1. that of speech production, of performance as opposed to competence;
2. that of hyperactivity and gross inattentiveness;
3. that of developing a program of cognitive stimulation and development for a diagnosed retarded child with manifest visual, auditory and attention weaknesses;
4. that of developing insights into the nature and meaning of diagnosed mental retardation.

THE AMELIORATION PROCEDURE

Since the child was diagnosed as "mentally retarded", any amelioration procedure had to be based on certain assumptions. The major assumption proposed was the concept of human abilities having "fluid boundaries". This concept implies that

(a) virtually any child may develop his abilities, however slowly, if there are at least no major neurophysiological constraints on such development. This negates concepts of "capacity" and "limits".

(b) endless interactions and associations may take place which differentiate one child's patterns of development from another. This negates the concept of "norms".

(c) the organism must cognitively assimilate aspects of the environment before it can meaningfully respond to those aspects as external stimulation. This is what McVicor Hunt (1967) has called the problem of match. In this context it implies that the environment must be presented in such a way that the child will perceive the environmental stimuli in the way that we want him to, and thus derive sense and meaning from the environment. This has particular implications for the development of reading behaviour.

In view of the four problems mentioned and the assumptions made in respect to the nature of human abilities four criteria were proposed in planning an amelioration programme.

1. that it should be stimulating and interesting and provide some control over attention and motivation. It was hoped to achieve this through a manipulation task since it was argued that manipulation helps to guide, focus and give direction;

2. that learning principles of instant reinforcement and control over possible errors should be built into the task without taking away the child's initiative;

3. that it should provide links between speech production, language development and reading stimuli which are the abstract representations of language;

4. that the programme should present the child with the task of visual sequencing and processing of orthographic stimuli represented in the form of words and letter signs. This meant that the child was to be confronted with the task of beginning to attach meaning to reading-type stimuli and the task of visually organizing these in preparation for reading behaviour.

Although his score on the I.T.P.A. subtest of visual reception placed him in the average category, the assumption that this implies visual readiness for

TABLE 3.2: Carl's matching responses to the model of his own name

Trial	Child's Responses
1	Therapist had to demonstrate
2	Therapist had to demonstrate
3	Therapist had to demonstrate
4	L r c a
5	L r c a
6	Had to be shown
7	C a r l

Three weeks later his matching ability was still very confused as the following pattern shows (after three demonstrations by the therapist).

the handling of reading-type stimuli is unjustified as the data in Tables 3.2 and 3.3 indicate. Carl was given a task involving the matching of the letters of his own name to a model of his name placed before him.

Three weeks later his matching ability was still very confused as the following pattern shows (after three demonstrations by the therapist).

TABLE 3.3: Carl's matching responses to the model of his own name after three weeks

Trial	Child's Responses
1	C a r l
2	C a r l
3	C a r l
4	A c r l
5	A c r l
6	I j j d
	Two further demonstrations were given at this point
7	C a r l
8	C a l r
9	C a r l *

* To help overcome this confusion the technique of superimposed matching already described in Research Report No. 2 was used. (See p. xx.)

At this point this task was discontinued though it was clear that his response of frustration to doing tasks was diminishing. The therapist noted: "he is now able to cope with the frustration of doing the task again and again."

The development of the rationale for this procedure and its implications for reading behaviour will be pursued under Apparatus "C".

THE METHOD EMPLOYED IN AMELIORATION

What follows is a description of the apparatus and method employed, samples of the child's responses to the task on varying occasions together with relevant comments. Essentially three kinds of apparatus were used.

Apparatus "A": Word-Object Inset Boards

Therapy began seriously in February 1970 and the boy was seen once a week for one hour. In order to meet the criteria already proposed a series of pieces of apparatus was constructed.

The first piece of apparatus consisted of bird and animal shapes and their "words" (i.e., the name of the animal) set in what have been called single frame inset boards. Thus both the animal, for example the shape of a cow, and the word "cow" on a little inset block could be taken out and matched in their respective places (see Figure 3.2). Initially the subject was presented with one puzzle at a time, told what it was, instructed to tip the animal or bird and its name out of the inset board and replace both shape and name, saying its name as he did so. This constituted practice in naming (verbalization) and identification (concept formation) together with the notion that there were words (concept symbols) which "belonged" to certain objects.

The series of concepts included such things as hen, duck, rabbit, tree, car, sheep, swan, rat, donkey, goat, dog, cow, koala. On 22.4.70 he was making the following vocalizations to the animal and bird cut-outs (see Table 3.4).

FIGURE 3.2

TABLE 3.4: The stimulus picture and the child's verbalizations

Stimulus animal cutouts	Child's verbalization
	22.4.70
Swan	War
Car	Ar
Horse	Hor
Dog	Dog
Sheep	Eep
Cow	Cow
Duck	Duck
Koala	Dala
Donkey	Dondon
Tree	Tee
Rabbit	Rab
Goat	Go

It was observed that when he held the therapist's hand he articulated the word better.

Two weeks later he was closer to pronouncing two more words: koala bear, to which he now responded "wala bear", and rabbit, to which he responded with "wabbit". A speech therapist was also giving him weekly practice in speech development. The fourth feature of the programme was to give him an orientation to reading stimuli which would prepare him for schooling.

Apparatus "B"

This apparatus was of the formboard type and consisted of pairs of shapes being presented to the subject. One shape of the pair had a left orientation and the other a right orientation (see Figure 3.3). He had great difficulty with the task as described in the therapist's notes of July 7, 1970. "When confronted with triangles facing in opposite directions he was greatly confused and took a long time to place the triangular pieces in their correct slots"; and "he took 3 trials to correctly place the b and d pieces in their respective spots and was confused over p and q."

Three weeks later however he appeared to have assimilated the nature of the task and could match most of the reversal inset pieces easily with the exception of the triangular shape which would take him as long as two minutes to achieve.

By the beginning of August 1970 however, he appeared to have mastered this task.

Apparatus "C": Analytic-Synthetic Word-Object Inset Boards

This piece of apparatus and method was designed to prepare Carl cognitively for reading behaviour and may therefore be seen as a pre-reading stimulation program. Since more work was done in this area than in any of the others the bulk of the remainder of this report will concentrate on the results of this programme.

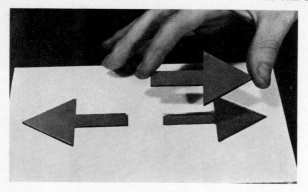

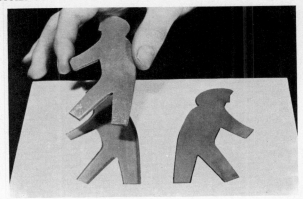

FIGURE 3.3

The apparatus consisted of a modular tile for presenting words in a simultaneous analytic-synthetic fashion. It contained an appropriate cut-out of a stimulus object together with two copies of its appropriate name. Thus if the stimulus object was "bus" there would be—

    (a) a cut-out object of "bus" which could be lifted out.

    (b) the word "bus", divided into its letter components at the top of the tile, which was the therapist's model, and

    (c) the word "bus", divided into its letter components at the bottom of the tile which was the sample for the child's use.

    (d) the words and their letters contained in a slot just big enough to house a three-letter word. This prevented the letter tablets from moving about and provided boundaries for perceiving the word. All letter tablets were identical in size and shape and therefore interchangeable.

FIGURE 3.4

(e) A line inscribed in the tablet under each of the letters thus instructing the subject which was top and bottom.

(f) The vowel symbols in the color red and the consonants in the color black.

An illustration of the tile may be seen by looking at Figure 3.4.

The instructions to the subject were as follows:

The modular tile was placed on the table in front of the child. The therapist then pointed to the bus object lift-out and said "this is a bus, say 'bus'." He handed the lift-out object to the subject asking him to replace it appropriately and say "bus" again, as he did so (language practice). The therapist pointing to the word bus at the top of the tile then said "this is the word for 'bus' " and, pointing to the one at the bottom said "this is your one", then returning to the one at the top said "this is my one, you can play with your one, but you musn't touch my one unless I tell you to". The therapist then took out the letter tablets of the word and instructed the subject to replace them and make "his one" just like the model one at the top of the tile. No mention was made at this stage of left-right sequencing.

The task had the following potential components for development:

1. a visual matching task where the S matched his letters to those of the model;

2. a visual sequencing task where the letters had to be arranged in correct order;

3. a visual concept formation task where the subject would attach a meaning to the entire collection of signs and confer unity on a word with its name;

4. a matching to memory task. This is essentially a spelling task where, after the child had learned to match to the exposed model correctly, the therapist's model would then be turned over so that the symbols were not visible and the child would then have to 'compose' the word with his tablets from memory. This would indicate whether he held a visual model of the word. He was able to check his effort for correctness by turning over the therapist's model and noting his own sample.

On 20.10.70 a consistent attempt was made to teach him the correct matching to model of three-letter words. The first word chosen was "pig", partly because of its potential difficulty, and partly because the author had done some work with this word with primitive New Guinea children from remote villages. His responses to that task together with the therapist's instructions are shown in Table 3.5.

Clearly the word "pig" was very difficult with its p and g similarities, so the word "cat" was selected, partly because he had a cat and partly because of the differences in the letter shapes.

Table 3.6 shows Carl's responses to the visual matching task using the word cat.

The session was concluded after 17 trials in which he was finally successful.

TABLE 3.5: Carl's matching-to-model responses using the word "pig"

Trials	Child's responses	Therapist's comments—after each attempt with child
1	i p g	"Put these together so they look like my one".
2	i b d	"You make your one the same as my one".
3	b i d	"We put them like this" (therapist takes tablets and demonstrates).
4	l g p	S changed it to g i p and therapist said "this one" pointing
5	g i p	to 'p' "comes first".
6	p i b	"Make it the same as my one".
7	i p g	"No, make it the same as my one".
8	g i p	"This one" pointing to 'p' "comes first", etc. "Now you make it like my one".
9	g i p	"You make it like my one".
10	g i p	

Clearly the word "pig" was very difficult with its p and g similarities, so the word "cat" was selected, partly because he had a cat and partly because of the differences in the letter shapes.

TABLE 3.6: The visual matching responses of Carl to the model word "cat"

Trial	Child's responses	T's responses and child's verbal responses
1	1 2 3* c a t	
2	2 3 1 c a t	
3	1 3 2 c a t	
4	1 3 2	"Is that the same as mine?" Subject said "Yes". Therapist
5	t a c	said "I don't think so, try again". "You make it the same as my one".
6	t a c	
7	1 3 2	(S screwed all the letter tablets up in his hand and threw them on the carpet and ran around the room. He spat, poked his tongue out, crawled under the table and lay on the floor. He was returned forcibly.
8	a t c	He then struck the apparatus with a letter tablet and knocked all of it on the floor. T. "Hurry up and put it back upon the table". S. "No…".
9	1 3 2 c a t	
10	2 3 1 t a c	T. "Do it again and make it like my one and hurry up". S. "No!" T. "That's not the same as my one". S. peered at "cat" and said "Peter, Peter, Peter, Peter (which was the name of his pet cat).
11	c a t	T. "Good, now let's try it again and make it like my word cat".
12	t a c	T. "No, make it exactly like my one".
13	c a t	
14	1 2 3 t a c	S. Self corrected it to c a t.
15	c a t	
16	c a t	
17	c a t	

*The numbers above the word refer to the order in which the letters of the word were matched.

The session was concluded after 17 trials in which he was finally successful.

By 7.12.70 Carl had achieved a considerable degree of competence in visual matching and could now match quite skilfully from memory as well. This latter task will be known as a "visual memory matching task". His responses after 8 sessions of matching practice spread over two months may be seen by reference to Table 3.7.

TABLE 3.7: Carl's visual matching-to-model responses and his matching-to-memory responses to three-letter words

Nature of word model presentation and No. of trials		Child's responses	Comments
	Word "pig" exposed		
	1	3 1 2 p i g	the "g" was self-corrected from upside down position.
	2	3 1 2 p i g	
	3	3 2 1 p i g	He was told how to sequence: which one to put "first".*
Visual Memory	4	1 2 3 p i g	
	Word "man" exposed		
	1	1 2 3 m a n	Very good.
	2	2 1 3 m a n	
	1	1 3 2 m a n	
Visual Memory	2	1 3 2 m a n	Very good
	Word "cat" exposed		
	1	1 3 2 c a t	Very good.
	2	1 3 2 c a t	
Visual Memory	1	2 3 1 c a t	S, "like that", and he pointed to the letter tablets.
	Word "pin" exposed		
	1	2 3 1 p i n	
	2	1 3 2 p i n	
Visual Memory	1	1 3 2 p i n	
	2	1 3 2 p i n	
	4	1 3 2 p i n	

*the term "first" was introduced after saying "we start here to make our words", pointing to the left-hand side.

Nature of word model presentation and No. of trials	Child's responses	Comments
Word "dog" exposed		
1	2 1 3 g o d	
2	1 2 3 d o g	T. "What's wrong with this fellow?"
3	g o d	S. self corrected to "god".
4 5	d g o 1 3 2 d o g	T. asked S. to look carefully which he did and corrected it to d g o.
6	1 2 3 d o g	He was then asked to look carefully again and try again.
Visual Memory 7 8	1 3 2 d o g 1 3 2 d o g	
Word "bed" exposed		
1	d e b	T. "Is your one the same as my one?"
2	2 3 1 b e d	
3	1 2 3 b e d	
4 5 7	d e b 2 3 1 b e d b e d	T. asked "does this one", pointing to "d", "look the same way as this one?" pointing to "b" in the model. S. looked and corrected it.
Visual Memory	2 3 1 b e d	

By this stage Carl would immediately check the correctness of the visual "matching from memory tasks", by turning over the therapist's model. This provided rapid visual feedback from which a correction could be made if necessary.

By August 1970 it was clear that Carl was imposing meaning and order on the specific visual environment to which he was being exposed; thus in September 1970 he was placed in the Monash Pre-School Centre to gauge his behavioural suitability for normal school placement. The teachers of the centre saw him as "a sort of average child without speech", who participated in and accepted the activities of the Centre. Contrary to past experience he did not beat other children up, nor was he particularly destructive.

By December 1970 his hyperactive behaviour had reduced itself to a minimum though he was at times still very difficult. His concentration on the visual matching tasks in the therapeutic sessions was such that he would stick to it under supervision for three quarters of an hour without showing signs of real frustration.

It was difficult for all concerned with the child to conceive of him even entering a normal school. The suggestion that he be given an opportunity to enter a normal school was viewed with apprehension and grave doubts about such a move were expressed by some. Since there was no prior model or experience for attacking such a problem, such apprehension was certainly not unjustified. However, despite this uneasiness in the minds of some, it was clear from the child's responses on the tasks which had been set for him, that cognitive structures had been built up which enabled him to attempt to cope with normal schooling.

It was felt therefore that it was worth trying to make such a placement. A letter was written to the infant school Principal explaining the nature of the problem. She was particularly helpful and willing to participate in the experiment. Thus in February 1971 he was sent to a "normal" school where he has been given every assistance by the class teacher and the infant school Principal. In March 1971 a more concerted effort was made to influence Carl's sequencing behaviour. His matching to model behaviour for the words "jam", "bib", "bus", and "fox" are illustrated in Table 3.8.

TABLE 3.8: Carl's sequencing and matching behaviour

Nature of word model presentation and No. of trials		Child's responses	T's comments
	Word "jam" exposed		
	1	1 2 3 j a m	
	2	1 2 3 j a m	
Visual Memory	1	1 2 3 j a m	
	2	1 2 3 j a m	
	"bib"		
	1	1 2 3 b i b	
	2	1 2 3 b i b	
Visual Memory	1	1 2 3 b i b	
	2	1 2 3 b i b	
	"bud"		
	1	1 2 3 b u d	

Nature of word model presentation and No. of trials		Child's responses	T's comments
	2	2 3 1* b u d	
Visual Memory	1	1 3 2* d u b	
	2	1 3 2* b u d	
	3	1 2 3 b u d	
"bus"	1	1 2 3 b u s	
	2	1 2 3 b u s	
Visual Memory	1	1 2 3 b u s	
	2	1 2 3 b u s	
"fox"	1	1 2 3 f o x	
	2	1 2 3 f o x	
Visual Memory	1	1 2 3 f o x	
	2	1 2 3 f o x	

It will be noticed that there was a relapse and some confusion experienced with the word "bud" where both sequencing and letter confusion became apparent.

It will be noticed that there was a relapse and some confusion experienced with the word "bud" where both sequencing and letter confusion became apparent.

The names of the sounds of some of the consonants was begun four weeks earlier and at this session he demonstrated that he could identify the sounds "b", "f", "s". A test of Carl's ability to recognize the words "fox", "jam", "bud", "bus" and "bib", showed that he could do so.

Writing of letters was also begun at this session. In order to aid his muscular control, which was very poor, he was introduced to the technique of tracing letters on a plastic screen with a model of the letter underneath. Then attempts were made to copy the letter. Copies of his attempts to write the word "dog" (a difficult task) showed that he could roughly approximate the word. On 5.5.71 and 11.5.71 his ability to recognize words (read) and his ability to pronounce them had increased considerably and this is illustrated by reference to Table 3.9.

Independent observers are quite satisfied along with his teachers that he is able to read the words although his pronunciation of them does not match those of a child with normal speech. Nevertheless it is easily recognizable with the words in front. It was reported that there were two or three who were worse than Carl at reading.

CONCLUDING COMMENTS

In all Carl has had approximately forty one-hour therapy sessions with highly structured materials designed to introduce him immediately to those kinds of skills which have a direct bearing on language development and reading stimuli.

The experimental procedure appears to have been successful in structuring those cognitive abilities essential for the beginning stages of formal education. His hyperactivity has virtually disappeared, his attention still wanders but *can* be captured and focussed on the task. His tolerance of frustration is quite high; his muscular control is still poor, but his reading behaviour is not greatly different from that of other preparatory children in the grade.

At this stage in the experiment we might well quote the words of A. D. Hope—"in the moment of success the heart stands still".

TABLE 3.9: Carl's ability to recognize and pronounce words

Word presented	Pronunciation and recognition
b u s	b u s
r u n s	r u
t o m	t o m
d o g	d o g
a n n	a (difficulty in pronouncing "n")

When the words Ann, Tom, runs, sits and stands were presented in a "line up" he correctly identified each word when spoken by the therapist. At this same time his teacher reported that he could recognize all of the words in the first book of the Happy Trio series and could pronounce them "in his own way".

The words of this book "We Look and See" are as follows:

Big Dick
Big Jane
Big Sport can work
Little Sally can play
Big big Jane
Little little puff
Play Sally play
Baby Sally can play.

Report No. 4

THE TACTICS OF AN UNEDUCATED REMEDIAL TEACHER

The tactics of an uneducated remedial teacher

The treatment of the reading disabled comes in varying ways and forms and is done by a variety of people. The following is a report on the strategies used by a father to teach his child to read.

Gay was seen on 17.12.69 for reading disability. She was then 9 years of age.

BRIEF HISTORY OF CHILD'S DISABILITY

Gay was born two months prematurely, and when she came home from hospital her parents noted that she had a fascination for light. She was a difficult child and began to bang her head on the cot, but the G.P. advised them that there was no need for worry as his daughter did the same.

At two and a half years the parents suspected there was something wrong with their child and she was admitted to the Children's Hospital where she was tested for suspected mental retardation. She remained in hospital for two weeks and at the end of that period the parents were informed that Gay was not greatly mentally retarded, but was minimally brain damaged.

She began school at five years of age and was promoted each year, her present placement being in Grade 3. Her behaviour had now settled down. Despite this, however, the father noticed that she was having difficulty learning to read and was encouraged to seek help because of a paper report on children who suffer from dyslexia.

REPORT ON PSYCHOLOGICAL TESTING

As a matter of routine inquiry the Weschler Intelligence Scale and the Daniels & Diack (1960) Standard Reading Test were administered to Gay. These results may be seen in Table 4.1. Her intelligence test results obtained from the administration of the Australian Revision of the Weschler placed her in the slightly mentally retarded category. Her reading age indicated that there was a marked reading problem and that she was functioning more like a child three years her junior. The exact nature of this difficulty is indicated by a further analysis of the kinds of errors she made.

Her performance on the Goodenough-Harris (1963) Draw a Man test however placed her in a category approximately one standard deviation above the average for her age and sex. Her drawings (see Figure 4.1 and Figure 4.2) correspond to her parents' and teachers' view of her as "somehow normal".

TABLE 4.1: Results of psychological testing

W.I.S.C. IQ	Daniels and Diack Standard Reading Test
Verbal 66 Performance 61 Full Scale IQ 60	Reading Age 6.2

On Test 4 of the Daniels & Diack Standard Reading Test, Gay made errors which revealed visual perceptual difficulty; she read:

b	for	d
Szwc	for	Swzc
loas	for	laos
peice	for	piece

On the consonant blend test, Test 7B, her confusions were legion, such as:

bag	for	brag	
load	for	clog	
gream	for	grim	
stamp	for	stop	
grab	for	glad	and so on.

Her father had set about to teach her to read when he discovered that she was having great difficulty, and the effectiveness of his method was demonstrated when 6 months later she appeared to be reading like a Grade 3 child rather than like a Grade 1 child.

FIGURE 4.1

FIGURE 4.2

The father was a building attendant, a semi-skilled workman who did not have a great deal of education himself, but who was determined that his child should, as he put it, "be able to earn her own living". His full-scale attack on Gay's reading disability was further motivated by the fact that on the one hand he thought she was "normal but lazy", and on the other, "dull". His normalcy perception appeared to dominate.

What follows is an example of a semi-skilled workman using rather skilled educational and psychological procedures without any training. It raises the old question: whether teachers are born and not made.

A tape recording was made of the father teaching his daughter.[4] His methods and procedures were then discussed with him and suggestions made as to where he might improve his technique.

The strategies used by the father appear in the left-hand margin, and the difficulties experienced by the girl and the father's interactions occur on the right-hand section of the page. The passage[5] which the girl was to read is printed here.

[4]The father co-operated happily in the interests of further research.
[5]The extract is taken from "The Third Reader", Education Department, of Victoria, p. 166.

The Golden Bird in the King's Garden

"There was once a king who had a beautiful garden. In it stood a tree that bore golden apples. About the time when the apples grew ripe, it was found that every night one of them was gone.

The king became very angry at this, and ordered the gardener to watch all night. The gardener set his eldest son to watch; but about twelve o'clock he fell asleep, and in the morning another of the apples was missing. Then the second son was ordered to watch; and at midnight he, too, fell asleep, and in the morning another apple was gone.

Then the third son lay down under the tree to watch. As the clock struck twelve, a bird of pure gold came; ...."

THE FATHER'S INTERACTIONS WITH THE GIRL TOGETHER
WITH THE TEACHING STRATEGIES USED

An Analysis of Techniques used By the Father to Teach his Daughter to Read.

The question form is used.

Gay began reading at the first sentence but the father believed that she should begin with the heading, so he asked "What's the name of the story?" She then turned to the heading and read correctly: "The Golden Bird in the King's Garden". She then commenced the story, reading, "There once lived a . . ." The father intervened with "You're leaving out a word" and proceeded to take her back to the beginning to retrace her steps hoping she would pick up the error. This she did and then read, "There was once a king". At this point the father praised her by saying: "Yeah, that's a girl".

Child put in a cognitive discovery set by using the technique of "retracing".

Use of praise.

In the next line of the passage Gay made a visual perception error and said "golden" for "garden". The father commented: "there's no golden, love" to which she responded with the correct word "garden", and the father signalled that she was correct with, "that's right".

A demonstration of how the sentence should be read is given.

Just two words further on she skipped over a full stop and thus did not get the sense out of the passage. This seemed to stimulate the father into producing a correct pattern of how the passage should be read, so he read it, pausing appropriately at the full stop.

Analyses elements of word to get child to deduce it.

At the next word Gay made a stab and said "boll" for "bore". The father analysed the word for her and asked "What sound does 'or' make?" She responded correctly and he praised her. She then attempted to attack the whole word and said "braul". The father intervened by saying, "you don't have to go 'br', there's no 'br' there— there's no 'r' after the 'b' is there? . . . it's just 'b' then 'or'." He then asked what the word was, hoping that Gay could string together the sounds, correctly deduced. Gay responded with "wor" to which the father said, "I beg your pardon?" She again said "wor". He felt she was not going to make it so he *informed* her: "It's just 'bore'."

Informs child of word.

She then proceeded to read "garten" for garden. Father interjected with "hum" which signalled to her that she had made an error. She tried again: "goeden", and then spontaneously had another try, "gar". He encouraged her to proceed in this direction by saying, "Yeah, that's right", and she then produced "garden". At this point the father said, "Now say the word again". She said it and he in turn said it, thus giving her a simultaneous double auditory and visual image.

Shaping behaviour.

Reinforcement practice.

The first word of the next sentence was "about" and when Gay looked at it she began to pronounce "p", to which her father responded, "No—it's not 'p' is it?" She responded now with a double, "pp" to which he replied, "No, it's not 'p'." She then corrected it to "b" and was told: "that's right."

Requests child to check her first impressions.

When Gay was reading well, he would attempt to keep up her confidence by interjecting, "that's right".

Keeps up the child's confidence.

In the second paragraph, Gay then read: "The king became very *ungry* (angry)", to which her father responded, "No, not ungry, you nearly got it right. That's just 'a', it's not 'u' in this case". She said it correctly and he commented "that's right".

The father uses a shaping technique to correct Gay and gives encouragement.

Further on in the passage Gay stumbled over the word "ordered" saying "old". Her father replied by drawing her attention to the first syllable "or" and saying "You know what 'or' is, we just said it before. When you're sounding out, what's the sound of 'or'?" The girl got this part correct and he attempted to boost her confidence by saying "You know that, that's right". She then continued to try the rest of the word: "orld, orld, orldered, orldered, orlder-ed". Her father responded, "that's right" and gave her the correct form, 'ordered'. In attacking the word "gardener" Gay said "gard, garder, garders, gard". The father asked, "Now what's the next bit?" She replied "en". "Yes", he said, "and what's the next bit?" She replied "er". Now the father asked "Now what is it?

Father draws attention to child's previously acquired knowledge and tries to give her a syllable attack procedure.

When she approximated the word, the father identified it as the correct word— when she had really been struggling.

*The father gives
a meaning clue by
asking a question
that will narrow
down Gay's
hypothesis about
what the word is.*

*A definition of
what reading is,
is offered. The
father explains
the two levels
of reading.*

*The father uses
the collective
term "We" so
that the girl feels
that she is not
alone in this
realm of
knowledge.*

What is he working at?" This was a sufficient clue and the child responded with "garden". Finally, by going over it again she came up with the full word "gardener". The father checked that she knew what a gardener was.

At this point Gay jumped a line, and the father took the opportunity to explain that reading is telling a story as well as just saying the words and sounding them out, and how "if you keep with the story and understand what the story's about, it helps you to read, doesn't it".

Earlier Gay had difficulty with the word "apples" and now she came across the word again but saying it correctly this time. The father recalling her earlier struggles with the word moved in quickly to impress the word on her mind by saying, "Yeah, that's right, you know they're apples Gay, that's right Gay, you take them to school nearly every day". Now the word "ordered" cropped up again to which Gay responded "old", more or less as before. The father reminded her that "*We* know what 'or' is" and Gay replied "orld". The father responded "that's right" and the girl said "orld, orlder, orlder". The father now replied "that's it, now hold onto 'o'. Look, we know that 'or' makes a certain . . . now what sound does it make? We'll have it again". Gay replied "or", to which the father added, "don't alter it, we've got that, now move onto the next part of the word". "Der" said Gay; "that's right" replied her father, and losing patience somewhat, "say 'ordered', Gay, 'ordered'." She responded, "ordered". He continued, "We've got the 'or', 'ordered', she 'ordered', he 'ordered' ", and then "Well you know what it is don't you?" "Yes". "You get ordered about at home sometimes don't you, and you get ordered about at school sometimes don't you?" "Yeah". "You know what the word means, alright, we'll start off here again".

Comment

This suffices to show the method employed. It involves well-founded techniques judiciously interwoven in a 15 minute teaching session.

In summary the techniques and procedures were as follows:
1.   Questioning to help the child think about the task.
2.   The use of personal discovery techniques and retracing of steps to aid picking up the error.
3.   The use of praise and encouragement as a reinforcer to learning.
4.   The use of demonstration. Where the adult felt it was important to give the child a well patterned overview, he did so by demonstration.

5. "Forcing" the child to analyse the word elements in order to deduce meaning.

6. Shaping of responses, used from time to time when he saw that the child was approximating the desired response and would achieve it with help.

7. A syllable attack method was encouraged, together with phonic emphasis.

8. The judicious use of meaning clues was employed when it was felt that this would help her search her memory for the correct form.

9. The father made sure she understood the meaning of a word with which she was having difficulty by relating it to her everyday experience.

10. Finally, the father evidences that he understands that reading may be defined at two levels, namely:

    (i) "it is saying words"
    (ii) "it is telling a story"

CONCLUDING COMMENT

A follow up study of Gay's reading ability two years later revealed that her reading skills were regarded as satisfactory by both the class teacher and the visiting school psychologist, as well as the parent.

In many instances the use of parents as teachers of their children is not only a failure, but also deliberately harmful. Yet there are numerous children who without the over-anxiety of their parents would not have made the kind of progress which they have made. Perhaps parents can be trained as remedial aides and assist the school programme with children other than their own, but who have similar difficulties. Secondly, where remedial assistance is not available, parents can doubtless be trained to be more effective in giving help to their disabled children.

REFERENCES

HARRIS, D. B.: *Goodenough-Harris Drawing Test Manual.* Harcourt Brace & World, 1963.
DANIELS, J. C. and DIACK, H.: *The Standard Reading Tests.* Chatto and Windus, London, 1960.

Report No. 5

THE PHANTOM

OF DYSLEXIA

The phantom of dyslexia

A young teacher said to me in a very special tone of voice: "I have a child in my class who is dyslexic". The teacher's tone of voice made me reply rather cryptically: "Well, aren't you just so lucky to have one of these rare specimens in your very own class!"

It then occurred to me that for some people it represents a great sense of achievement to identify, diagnose and classify a series of discrete and discrepant child behaviours under one foreign summary term. It appears to generate psychologically a penetrating sense of comfort and relief in the teacher, parent or diagnostician. It is as though classification is the important goal; the rest does not matter. Some people do not appear to have the overt aspect of the term quite straight in their mind; an earnest young thing asked me whether she might talk to me about her niece who had "dysexia" ..... I hesitated for a moment and earnestly enquired: "I beg your pardon, but what did you say?" There was a moment of faltering recognition; she wasn't quite sure. "You know, dysexia", she ventured. Did she have a niece who somehow couldn't perform the sexual act, or was she somehow deprived of part of her sexual organs? Of course I knew what she was talking about, but I found myself muttering, "dysexia, dysexia, dys, dy . . . ." and my thoughts jolted me into a kind of fury as I thought of just another child imprisoned and enshrined for ever in the tomb of dyslexia. I wondered whether a child who had been a chronic reading disability case and whose disability had been resolved was still "dyslexic"? I tried to think of an analogy. Was a person who had cancer, but who had recovered after surgery, still a cancer case? The answer seemed to be "No". But then the cancer patient had something physically identifiable. She had a disease which could in certain cases be seen and excised; but what of dyslexia: does the child "suffer from it in the same way?" Is it a thing that can be viewed, and perhaps at a later stage excised? Clearly the answer seemed to be "No"! The analogy does not seem to fit; it leads us completely astray if we take a medical model viewpoint when considering chronic reading disability, or so-called Dyslexia.

Reading is a process, not a thing. Of course physiological, neurophysiological, neurochemical and biochemical factors may either facilitate, interfere with, or impede the process; faulty vision, faulty hearing and the like are typical examples. But it must never be forgotten that reading is the process of making sense out of visual symbols which in themselves are among the most variable stimuli man has yet been called upon to deal with.

In so many ways learning to read just does not follow the usual laws of learning. These laws include such basically established principles as (1) learning a link between a particular response to a particular stimuli; (2) learning the principle of generalization of the response to similar examples and classes of stimuli; and (3) learning clearly defined discriminations that a particular stimulus rarely alters in a basic sense.

Learning to read defies all of these principles. For example, the child has to learn that when he hears the sound "f" as in "if", it may be written in many different ways such as "f" as in "if", "ff" as in "off", "lf" as in "calf", "gh" as in "laugh", "ph" as in "graph", "fe" as in "safe". The lack of principle holds for numerous other sounds. To take another example, "ch" as in "school", "qu" as in "mosquito", "que" as in "antique", "ke" as in "cake". The long vowel sound a has ten different spellings; "i" has fifteen different spellings, and so on.

As if this is not enough to confuse the child, a second inconsistency appears. When you look at the visual symbols themselves and attempt to read them back there are many differences such as—"c" in the initial position of a word has the sound of "k" as in "kid"; if it is followed by some vowels it has the sound of "s" as in "city"; but when followed by other vowels this does not hold, thus although the "c" in "cat" is followed by the vowel "a", it has the sound "k". There is a rule which says " 'c' has the sound 'k' except when it is followed by e, i, or y, when it usually says 's'." Then there are letters which make no sound. This problem arises after teaching the child that they do make a sound! Letters such as "k" in "knee" and "knit", "y" in "say", "g" and "u" in "laugh", and so on.

It must be pointed out also that when the child hears "hw" as in "when" he must unlearn the well-established sequencing rule which says if you *hear* the sounds in a temporal order you must *write* them in a temporal order, as in "cat". But when he hears "hw" as in "when" he must write "wh" and not "hw".

Lest one imagine that that is all, it is needful to indicate that when some vowels occur together as in "boat", "seat", "rain", the first one alone is sounded and the second is silent; but when the child is beginning to get that confusion unconfused he is confronted with the fact that for "au", "ou", "ui", "eu", "as", and "oy", this is not the case; they have special sounds depending on the special circumstances. Contrary to the views of Gestalt Psychology, simple words are neither easily nor systematically perceived. Each individual tends to interpret stimuli according to his own particular history, and what one person sees in a situation another may not see, or may see only after prolonged instruction. The perception of words is quite different, for example, from the perception of many objects and creatures. Creatures such as cats, horses and the like in the child's environment are seen for what they are fairly soon. No one ever heard of a child looking at a horse in the paddock and, for example, "reading" it upside down, or back to front. This is due to the fact that the stimulus is a unified, integrated whole. The legs move, the head moves, the tail moves, the body moves, the whole creature moves. There is never a situation where the legs of a cow are fitted to a dog, or the tail of a horse to a cat, for instance. Furthermore children grow to experience such creatures through at least four sensory channels; they hear them, they see them, they smell them, they touch them. In reading, however, the bits of a word can be taken away and recombined, presumably into a fantastic array of combinations. For example, it is possible to visually process the word "pig" in no less than 192 different ways. These ways are the result of order variation processes, reversal and order variation processes and inversion variations and order, reversals and inversions combined. Some of the following combination processes, produced by primitive New Guinea native children from the Eastern Highlands who had never been to school, indicate the method of visually reproducing the word "pig", and classifying it in the same way as "pig". "pig, pgi, igp, gpi, ipg, gip, dig, dgi, igd, gdi, idg, gid, piᵷ, pᵷi, iᵷp, ᵷpi, etc. . . ." When five-letter words are considered, the child may produce as many as 123,280 variations in visual processing! This has become apparent from recent work which the author has done on primitive native children who have not been confronted with an environment which has any orthographical symbols at all (see Figure 5). The implications of this appear to be that the elements of each word have to be carefully presented from a stable reference point, so that children lay essential conceptual building blocks and learn to play the game of reading as we play it.

Furthermore, it has been demonstrated by this author that, as the physical structure of the word varies, so does the child's tendency to process it vary. For example, I have demonstrated that for a small sample of bright children, just prior to entering school, the word "truck" is processed consistently from right to left, with some confusions within the word itself. However, when the same group of children were presented with the word "pig" no such consistent mode of visual processing occurred. New Guinea children, who have never been confronted with English orthography, visually process the word "pig", for example, significantly more often from right to left rather than from left to right as we want children to do in English. That any children in fact master the reading and spelling of a language with so many confusions ought to be wondered at, rather than that they do not learn.

Since there are virtually an infinite number of visual processing errors that may take place by a young child in sorting out and making sense of English orthography, and since once an error has been well embedded according to well-established laws of learning, the process of unlearning and change may be a very formidable one indeed.

In an age when less formal and precise teacher training is done for the infant teacher, rather than more formal and more precise work, the number of reading problems is likely to increase greatly, not because of any constitutional disability in children, but because of a glossing over of and lack of insight into the beginning reading process.

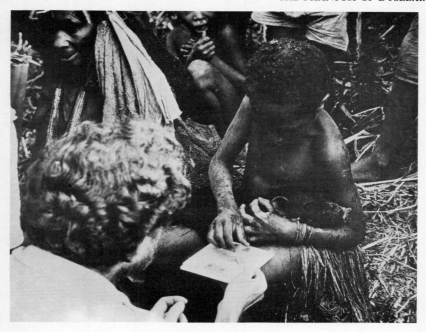

FIGURE 5.1

It is sometimes argued that remedial reading procedures would be different if it could be shown that in one case the cause was organic and that in another it was non-organic. Herein lies the fallacy; for one is not concerned with modifying organicity but with the modification of cognitive structure, whatever the origins of its immediate incompetence.

Reading is an environmentally induced process. It is dependent of course on the wired-in nature of the organism, but it is environmentally induced nevertheless.

In some quarters there seems to be a preoccupation with the dichotomy between neurological and environmental causes, leading to some rather strange pronouncements. Thus some for example have said that if the cause is emotional the treatment will be psychotherapy, aided when possible by preventive sociological action; and if the cause is neurological the treatment will be remedial teaching. One might have thought that if the cause were neurological the treatment should have been neurosurgery rather than remedial teaching.

All of this seems to ignore the central and crucial variable in learning to read: the reading stimuli itself and how this is processed by children. Thus when two children face the task of making sense out of orthographic stimuli for the first time and one succeeds and the other does not, we cannot assume that both children are processing the visual material in the same way. Some of the ways in which children visually process orthographic stimuli have been reported by Gibson (1970). The findings reported in this present paper, however, look at the problem in a new way. The only way to conceptualize the nature of reading behaviour is to look more closely at the perceptual, cognitive and stylistic modes of 1. visual processing of orthographic stimuli, 2. auditory processing of phonemes, and 3. memory storage and output systems.

In a recent preventative programme the present author has taken two groups of eight Grades 1 and 2 primary school children who were exhibiting the classical symptoms of reading disability, reversals, sequencing errors, reversals, mirror imagery and the like. The Grade 2 children in particular were doing this despite "normal" teaching and "normal" home environment. After twelve months of remediation treatment with the older group, working with them in groups of eight and using procedures based on principles evolved from this author's research on visual processing, all but one of the children overcame their basic difficulties. The Grade 2 group, whose mean age was $7\frac{1}{2}$ years, made gains in reading of between 9 and 19 months, with a mean gain of $13\frac{1}{2}$ months. The second group of Grade 1 children whose ages ranged from 6 years 3 months to 6 years 11 months, and whose mean age was 6 years 3 months and with whom preventative treatment was initiated only six months ago, made gains ranging from 1 month to 12 months with a mean gain of 4 months. It is to be noted that this was a group remediation programme and if such gains could be made with a group programme it is assumed that much more could be expected with a more individualized treatment programme.

This discussion has centred on the problems inherent in English orthography and on the visual processing done by children. If valid, it should alter considerably our perspectives about reading disability and make us extremely cautious about labelling a child as dyslexic. This need for caution is further illustrated by the case of a five and a half year old girl "diagnosed" as dyslexic and referred for further consideration. She had the usual symptoms of hyperactivity, distractability and confusions with symbols at school, very poor motor coordination and poor eye-hand coordination. When confronted with the task of visually processing the

TABLE 5.1: The steps involved in a five and a half year old diagnosed dyslexic child's visual processing of the word "pig" to criterion of three errorless trials

Test trial	Child's visual processing once with stimuli exposed	Test trials	Child's visual processing response from memory
1	dig	9	pgi
2	dgi	10	dig
3	igd	11	pig
4	pig	12	pig
5	pig	13	pig
6	pgi		
7	pi		
8	pig		

word "pig", for example, she took 8 trials before her mode of processing conformed to the way in which it is expected to be done by readers of English. Table 5.1 shows the steps involved in the processing.

The question must be asked: was this child dyslexic? She showed all the symptoms. After ten minutes remediation treatment with specialized treatment apparatus she played the game of reading as we all do, for three consecutive trials at any rate! Can she now be considered dyslexic if she reveals few errors or no errors after brief treatment?

The pointless use of such a label was significantly reflected recently by the dilemma of a young teacher who had taken a child into her grade, referred to her by a child specialist and diagnosed as dyslexic. She mentally noted the symptoms: inattentive, distractable, hyperactive, left-handed, problems with reading, and so on. A close look at the boy showed that he certainly exhibited the symptoms, but after eighteen months of educational therapy his reading and spelling errors had become quite minor. Despite such a recovery, however, the teacher clung to her diagnosis and would refer in conversation, to her case of dyslexia.

Labelling does not help the academic therapeutic process. Spectacles may help, lessened emotional tension may help, increased motivation to learn may help, perceptual training may help, but more importantly, as Cohen (1970) has pointed out, close attention to the independent variables of visual and auditory discrimination of letters and words, which after all are operationally closest to the dependent variable of reading, is of crucial significance if we are to aid the disabled reader. Even more crucial is a consideration of the nature of visual processing of orthographic stimuli by children. This seems to be the parent of visual discrimination and it is to this activity we must look if we are to help children unravel the agreed set of rules of visual processing orthography in the English-speaking environment, irrespective of the cause of their disability.

REFERENCES

COHEN, S. A.: Cause Versus Treatment in Reading Achievement. *Journal of Learning Disabilities,* Vol. 3, No. 3, March 1970, pp. 43-46.
GIBSON, E.: The Ontogeny of Reading. *American Psychologist,* Vol. 25, No. 2, February 1970.

POSTSCRIPT

TOWARDS A THEORY OF DYSLEXIA

From the observations made on children with chronic reading disability, as instanced in the reports in this book, and on primitive native children's strategies for coping with the initial confrontation with reading stimuli, the historical cause of reading disability in a particular case appears to be largely irrelevant to reading remediation procedures.

What do appear to be relevant, however, are the following observations:

1. that chronic reading disability is largely a case of mis-assimilation and mis-organization of reading stimuli.
2. that this mis-assimilation and mis-organization becomes thoroughly embedded in the early stages of confrontation with reading stimuli and represents the subject's cognitive framework through which he views subsequent manifestations of those stimuli.
3. that the mis-assimilation and mis-organization is learned according to well-established and well-organized laws of learning.
4. that this thoroughly learned process of mis-assimilation and mis-organization becomes the thing called dyslexia or chronic reading disability.
5. that this mis-assimilation and mis-organization may be facilitated by—
   (a) a neurophysiological structure that makes the capture of attention, memory and other factors somewhat difficult, and
   (b) socioemotional factors which contribute to a lack of the appropriate mental set towards reading, and
   (c) brain damage factors and a number of other variables, but most importantly by faulty presentation of reading stimuli to the child.
6. that the disability is preventable and remediable by the appropriate techniques, some of which have been outlined in this book and other have yet to be published.

The final observation indicates that all children ought to be "immunized" against acquiring the disability within the first year of school. This programme could cost money, but it would be money well spent at the right end of the problem.